Pragmatic Psychology

Practical Tools for Being Crazy Happy

Susanna Mittermaier

ACCESS
CONSCIOUSNESS®
PUBLISHING

Pragmatic Psychology
Copyright © 2013 Susanna Mittermaier
ISBN: 978-1-939261-27-4

Cover photo: Lena Evertsson

Published by
Access Consciousness Publishing, LLC
www.accessconsciousnesspublishing.com

Printed in the United States of America

Contents

INTRODUCTION

Writing this book was an amazing journey and a pleasure! I am supposed to say that it was hard work and that it took me a long time. I would be lying. It was easy and fast. Just like me.

I am presenting to you what I know and inviting you to find out what you know. What if you know way more about you and about creating the life you truly would like than you thought? What if the things you call wrongness and crazy and insane are exactly the tools to access your happiness and the joy you be. What if you started to celebrate the difference you be?

GRATITUDE

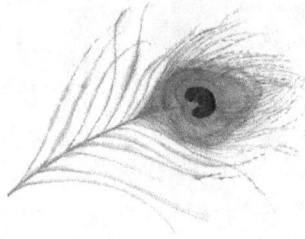

My gratitude is huge! Thank you, Gary M. Douglas, the man who keeps acknowledging who I be and what I am truly capapble of. Thank you for being and living the greater reality that is available on this planet and for never giving up! Thank you, Dr. Dain Heer, the man that tickles me into the joy and potency I be and keeps reminding me that my reality truly is ease, joy and glory. Thank you mum and dad. You are such kind people! Having you as parents is the greatest honor. Thank you for supporting me to be who I be.

Thank you, Joy Voeth for your publishing service and for the joy and ease creating with you. And thank you so much everybody involved in editing and design.

Thank you readers for considering greater possibilities for You.

Enjoy the read.

Enjoy You.

Susanna Mittermaier

Pragmatic Psychology: Practical Tools for Being Crazy Happy

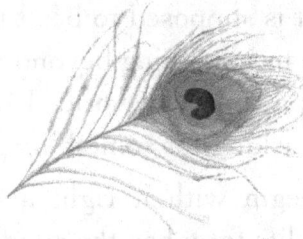

🖝 Is now the time to create the world we always knew was possible?

🖝 What if living can be much lighter and easier than you thought it could be?

🖝 What if you could let go of every "wrongness" of you, all the doubt about everything you cannot achieve, all the judgments you have of yourself and become aware of who you truly are and what you are truly capable of?

🖝 Is now the time to getting over being weighed down by your past?

🖝 What if psychology could be more than fixing problems? What if psychology could be about empowering you to be everything you are and you knowing what you know? What if psychology coud be about creating a different, sustainable future for you and all of us?

☞ What reality that has never existed before are you now capable of generating and creating for yourself and the world?

☞ Is now the time to enjoy and employ your crazy to create the life you truly desire?

☞ Is now the time for you to be crazy happy?

❋ ❋ ❋

Funny, I just noticed that I started this book by writing about the part that is supposed to be at the end, the grand finale, inviting you to something beyond the limitations you thought were real; a different world. I figure if you chose this book, you are asking for something greater.

So why not begin with it right away? Haven't you waited your whole life for when the good part starts? What if the happy ending is available *now*, and what if it is just the beginning?

What if you could stop making yourself wrong for desiring something greater, beyond what this reality seems to offer and what others say is possible? Do you know what a gift you are to the world just by being you, and asking for something more?

Most people have been judged for never being satisfied. Asking for more is what sets the world in motion. It is what allows for new possibilities to show up beyond the limitations that others make real.

How much of your life are you using to solve problems and issues? How much are you trying to feel good as though that was the result you are supposed to achieve? And how bad have you felt your whole life for not getting to the point where you felt good enough? How much are you judging yourself on a daily basis for not getting it right, doing enough, being enough, for not having the right body, the perfect relationship, the money, the great sex, the successful career and business? How many times in your life were you hit by depression, anxiety, panic attacks or other not-so-pleasant expressions and felt trapped with no way out?

This is the reality the majority of people live in. It's a world where depression, anxiety and other diseases are a regular part of life. Feeling bad and having problems is considered normal in this reality! How many of your problems are you creating to be normal? What if you could get over being normal and tap into the true brilliance of you?

* * *

I am a clinical psychologist and I have been working in mental health for the past years and have met countless amounts of people with all kinds of diagnoses and issues. What they all tell me is how terrible they are; that they have all kinds of problems and they never do it right or fit in anywhere they go. They say they would like to change, but they do not think change is a possibility because they have tried so many techniques and therapies and nothing has really worked. Sometimes I meet people where it has gone so far that they have stopped talking. Others have tried various medicines, but none had the desired effect.

My clients have diagnoses such as: depression, anxiety, schizophrenia, phobias, eating disorders, personality disorder, bipolar, ADHD (attention deficit hyperactive disorder), ADD (attention deficit disorder), OCD (obsessive compulsive disorder), autism, Asperger's and variations thereof.

I work with these people in a very different way than what I have learned to do in my education to become a psychologist. I was never really happy with the tools I was handed and I have always known that something greater is possible. So I started a journey to find a way of facilitating change that works. What I found was Access Consciousness®, founded by Gary M. Douglas and co-created by Dr. Dain Heer.

Access Consciousness® offers tools and techniques to change whatever is going on in your life so you can get out of the trap of thinking there is no choice but to be burdened by the wrongness of you, and get to a place where you know you have choice—where you know what you know and where you feel free to be who you truly are. This is the space where you are home, creating your world. This way of creating change is truly different.

Now let's begin!

CHAPTER ONE

HOW I HAD IT ALL WRONG

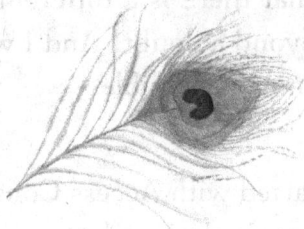

I know from my own experience about the challenges of personal transformation. Despite my outward success, 5 years ago I realized how unhappy I was. I had everything a person in this world should have to be totally happy and satisfied—an education, a nice man, money, a house, a job, a blossoming career and I was pregnant. I looked around at my neighbors and said to myself: "Why can't I be as happy as these people? I have everything. What is wrong with me?"

Shortly after that, my whole world twisted around me. I remember getting back from the doctor and receiving the news that I had a dead baby in my belly. It was quite late in the pregnancy and I stood in the living room in my perfect house, and my perfect life crumbled right in front of me, and literally the lights went on. I had one of those weird experiences where I saw white light around me...and I knew all was well. I was happy!

I was not supposed to be happy knowing that I lost everything I thought I wanted. Yet soon I began creating a much greater reality—the death of my child birthed a life that I did not know was possible for me to have on this planet!

Now I know that there is a different possibility for all of us! I know it beyond a doubt! And I would like to invite you to what you know is possible.

❊ ❊ ❊

When I first started with Access Consciousness®, I realized that psychology is designed to make your life better while still fitting into this reality, making you a better version of who you were before; to fit in, it is required that you change your way of thinking and behaving.

This approach does not leave a lot of freedom as it is always based on judgments of what is the right way to be and live, and what is the wrong way to be and live. It leaves you at the place where you constantly have to figure out what to choose to be right, to fit in and to be "normal."

However, I began to wonder: Is this enough? Is that working? What do my clients really know?

I am inviting you to something different, where I will not tell you what is right or wrong or what you should do or not do. I am inviting you to ask questions and to find out what is true for you.

When I embarked on this journey, I was stunned to find out that life can be so much more expansive than trying to fit in and be normal. I always knew that happiness is a choice we all have. Becoming an adult I forgot about that possibility as I was so busy trying to create a "normal" life. Everything seemed so picture-perfect, yet I was slowly getting more and more depressed living someone else's version of life.

How much of your depression, anxiety and other problems are about you living someone else's version of life, and about you knowing there is so much more available for you that you never allowed yourself to choose? How much is about being told that what you find possible, is not possible? Or being told, with or without words, that you are crazy for even considering something different? How much have you listened to these statements, making yourself wrong, holding back everything you know is true for you, creating pain, tension, depression and psychological problems, and locking them into your body?

Is now the time to change that?

What if you acknowledged what is true for you could change your whole life and more?

Acknowledging who I am and what I know is what changed my life from depression mode to fantastic superspeed creation mode with a great deal of happiness.

Are you ready to get over your perceived problems and what you thought was real and find out what possibilities and adventures are waiting for you?

I have to warn you: It is crazy and it is easy. Two things that are not allowed in this reality. Are you ready to break the rules?

* * *

You might wonder about the title of this book and what psychology has to do with creating your world. And why "world"—isn't that kind of big? Yes, it is. What if being you is a gift to the world? What if getting out of the wrongness of you and creating your living would not only change your world, but would also be the invitation for others to choose, and for others to know that they know and be who they be?

I have seen this occur with so many of my clients. They choose to be more of who they truly are and their whole reality changes. Every time I choose to step up and celebrate living and the difference I am, my reality and the people around me change.

I used to try to make my parents happy and did all I could to show them that life can be so much greater than drama and trauma and thinking that everything they do is wrong. The more I tried to make them happy, the unhappier I became. When I started to enjoy my happiness, they started to ask me questions about what I do to be so happy. They became interested in learning more about the tools I use. They even started coming to the workshops I facilitate and telling me every time they learned something new. Now they know they have choice in every moment, and I know I have choice to be in allowance of what they choose.

This book is an invitation for you to step out of the box you call your life; to let go of the judgments that limit you and the things you call your problems so that you can be who you truly are and generate and create your reality as you truly wish.

How different would your world be if you would drop the "wrongness" of you, the significance of your problems, and realize what is true for you?

You might call me crazy for having such a point of view. And you would be correct; I am. What if being crazy is what allows us to be the difference we truly are and what if it allows us to realize that there is a different possibility for all of us and the world? What if allowing you to be crazy and different means not having to work so hard fitting in and being like everybody else and trying to be "normal" anymore? Are you aware of how much energy it takes to try to be normal and fit in?

What if every "wrongness" you think you have is really a "strongness"? What if the freak you think you are is actually the difference you are—and what if that is exactly what the world requires of you? What if your so-called mental illness is simply a label of the capacities you have? Would you be willing to consider that as a possibility? Are you willing to give up your points of view about who you thought you were and start the adventure of finding out who you truly are? What do you know is actually possible for you?

Are you willing to open up to a different possibility?

What if you have a different choice other than being the victim of your story, your past, your childhood and your problems? What if you have the possibility to choose something different? And what if it was way easier and quicker than anybody ever told you?

This book will give you the information, tools and keys to your freedom beyond what you call your problems and issues and beyond your necessity to limit yourself.

When I attended high school I was considered not as smart as the other children. The term used was "not as gifted." But at university I was one of the best students. This did not make sense to me so I asked myself, "What is truly going on? What is the awareness here that I have not acknowledged?" What I discovered is that what was called a "disability" was merely a sign that I process information differently. I learned that what was considered a "wrongness" is actually a difference that I can use to my advantage, since it allows me to process a lot of information in a short amount of time and with total ease. Before I started asking questions to find out what is true for me, I made myself the effect of my childhood and thought that I was stupid. Through asking questions, a totally different world opened up.

What ability have you misidentified as a disability?

What if you are so much more than your problems, thoughts, feelings and emotions?

What if you could employ your so-called mental illness to your advantage? Welcome to the superwoman and superman *you truly are*.

Many of my clients tell me they would have liked to have received this information when they were young, since it could have changed their whole life.

I am not your expert or guru. I am here to invite you to find out what you already know. When you read this, be aware of what makes you feel lighter and what expands your universe. What makes you feel lighter is what is true for you.

Is now the time to find out what you know?

Is now the time to trust yourself?

✳ ✳ ✳

Susanna — The Weird Psychologist

For years I have been working as a clinical psychologist, using different kinds of methods; for example long- and short-term psychodynamic therapy and cognitive behavioral psychotherapy. I apply neuropsychological testing to ascertain diagnoses.

In my first year as a clinical psychologist, my work felt heavy and my body was often tired. I had the point of view that it was my responsibility to take care of my patients, to make them better and to save them from committing suicide.

Would you like to close the book now and go to sleep? Well, that is how my first year as a psychologist was. Work and sleep. And for many of my colleagues this is still the reality they are living in. This might sound exaggerated, but look around. How much energy do most psychologists, social workers, teachers, mothers, fathers, etc. have after a week of work? How much time are people using to save others and to make others feel better?

How much time do you use to make others feel better? Scan through your life and get the sense of how much of your time is used to help others.

I was not even aware of how much energy my work cost me. Yes, I use the word "cost" on purpose. We pay not only in money, we also pay with our time, our energy and ourselves. After only one year I started considering a different profession. I was not willing to commit my life to just hard work and sleep. No way! The results I was getting with the traditional ways of doing therapy were not good enough to keep on working the way I did. What I could facilitate for my clients was not what I knew was possible.

This had to change! That was my demand. Even if I had studied many years to become a psychologist, I was willing to let it all go and look for a different profession if the work and the way it showed up did not change.

During that time, I had the awareness that an education would change things for me. Some kind of course or workshop would be the starting point for something new. I did not know what kind of course or when it would show up. I just knew that it would. The knowing was strong.

Please, don't have any fun reading this book. Fun is bad. It is immoral and makes life way too easy. Especially being a psychologist and working with therapy one ought to be very serious, otherwise one will be judged and hung on the cross of a non-scientifically evidence-based being. We have to be "professional." Being professional means excluding fun. The greatest change occurred with my clients when they started allowing themselves to have fun.

Oh, to satisfy my brain, which for a large part of my life was my dearest asset. My brain and I were the best of friends; we would do anything together, go anywhere, solve any problem…oh, those were the days.

So yes, I was a "brainfooter." What is a "brainfooter?" You know, when young children start drawing people, they draw them with a big head and tiny feet attached to the brain. They do not draw that way because they have a limited capacity of drawing at that age. In fact, they are brilliantly aware of how people choose to function in this reality. They know this is a brain-only world. Leave your body behind, take your brain and let's rock and roll. I call that way of functioning being a brainfooter: brain on feet. (Welcome to my weird sense of humor.)

OK, back to where I was. To satisfy my overly active brain, I constantly looked for workshops and trainings. My brain demanded me to do something, since just trusting and being and allowing it to show up was not enough for my dear brain. I had to be in control. (By the way, do you know anything about being a control freak yourself?)

My diligent search was to no avail. Then an Access Consciousness® workshop showing up at a time and in a way I least expected. I had no idea what it was about, but I went, knowing somehow it would change my life.

The workshop lasted five days and it led me to attend other Access Consciousness® workshops and classes all over the world: Sweden, England, Costa Rica and Australia. The result: I felt I had a totally different life, a different reality and a suitcase filled with tools to facilitate change for me and the world.

My relationship changed. I sold my house and moved to the city. I changed my way of working, and most of all, I had a sense of me and what I am truly capable of that I never thought was possible.

Now I am creating a different paradigm with psychology and therapy, with what I know and am and with the revolutionary tools of Access Consciousness®. I call it, "Pragmatic Psychology."

CHAPTER TWO

PRAGMATIC PSYCHOLOGY

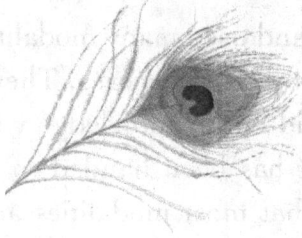

W hat do I mean by "Pragmatic Psychology?" It's my name for the techniques, information and perspectives that facilitate you to get out of being the victim and the effect of your past, other people and your conditioning. These tools empower you to know that you have choice; utilizing them opens the door for you to create your life and to live the way you truly desire. Pragmatic Psychology acknowledges your capacities, who you are and what you know. It is about getting everything out of your way that does not allow you to be you. Pragmatic Psychology is applying the tools of Access Consciousness® to psychology and therapy to create a different perspective on insanity, diagnosis and a greater possibility for change.

This is not another theory or concept that tells you how you should live your life. It is not a recipe for how to fix your life. Nor is it a modality that tells you what is right and what is wrong. It is not about getting you to adapt more to this reality. Most modalities and theories are designed to achieve all that—they are a way of explaining and making understandable what is going on in the world as an attempt to find a solution to suffering and pain. How many of those modalities have you tried? Did they work for you?

I have studied and used many modalities and they never gave me a sense of peace and ease. They never gave me a sense of me and did not acknowledge what I know is possible beyond what has been handed to me as this reality. What I found is that most modalities are created to fix a problem, which means that people who use these modalities assume that there is a problem.

Clients assume this too. When I meet with them everyday, they tell me all they went through, all the abuse, and how wrong they are, and it brings tears to my eyes. I see their brilliance, their capacities, their amazingness, and the difference they are that they have not yet acknowledged, which is their capacity to change the world.

I always knew that a different way of facilitating change is possible. I created Pragmatic Psychology so people can start acknowledging who they truly are and start switching on the lights of awareness.

Pragmatic Psychology provides the tools, the information and the expansion of your awareness that allow you to know what you know, receive everything without judgment, and change everything you desire to change.

Psychology used to be the art of knowing. Later it became the study of behaving and thinking. What if we could create psychology as the empowerment for you to know that you know?

Pragmatic Psychology takes psychology out of the polarity of this reality, where everything is about good and bad and right and wrong, doing the right thing, making the right decision, winning and not losing. Psychology in the traditional sense is about adapting and fitting into this reality as well as possible. It sets the guidelines for what is sane and insane. It posits that having a psychological problem is right and "normal."

Most of the time psychology does not even question whether you really do have a problem. Instead, it is about looking for what is wrong, assuming that there is something wrong and why it is wrong and looking for evidence that there is something wrong.

On the other hand, Pragmatic Psychology invites you to question, to have choice, possibility and encourage contribution. It invites you to a place where you get out of the wrongness of you to where you know that you have choice, and where you ask the questions that create greater possibilities for you and your life, and where you contribute to the creation of what you truly desire. By asking questions you move beyond answer and conclusion into the awareness about what is truly possible for you.

Problems and difficulties are created only when we are not willing to be aware and when we are not willing to see what is. Every time we diminish our awareness and are not willing to be conscious, we create problems. It is kind of like trying to get dressed in the dark. What you find wearing when you get into the light might not be what you hoped for.

Many times what is really going on for people is too weird for this reality, which makes most people stay in the range of normality where you come up with some kind of answer as to why a problem is not changeable, or it is just concluded that the person is too sick to be cured. Examples of this are schizophrenia and autism. Many experts do not really know, or even want to know what is truly going on with people with these diagnoses because what is truly going on is beyond the "normality" of this reality. I have met patients with psychosis and schizophrenia and when we looked at what was really going on, even if it did not fit any explanation model in psychology, it changed their lives and they no longer fit the standard diagnosis.

To know what is, is called awareness. It is turning on the lights to see what is. When you turn on the lights you see everything. You no longer have to step into broken glass on the floor of your life and you can see where there is grass that is nurturing to walk on. To expand your awareness about what is really going on, it takes asking questions and not coming to conclusions and trusting your knowing. It is like being a detective. What you find is way beyond what this reality finds possible.

Psychology was originally supposed to be a tool to get you free from the ego but it is an incorrect description of what is. Is the ego real or a creation? The ego is a concept that is created by the mind. People are trying to get free from something that is an invention. Like every other problem. So people are trying to get free from their mind by using their mind, the very thing that creates the problem. How well is that working? How many things that are not even real are you trying to get rid of when all you do is go further and further down the rabbit hole and into your own invention?

What if psychology could be about you being as conscious as you truly are? Consciousness is very pragmatic.

It gives you the information you require to create what you truly desire.

> *"Consciousness includes everything and judges nothing."*
> ~ Gary M. Douglas

Pragmatic Psychology is about asking questions to find out what is, instead of what the mind *thinks* is going on. It is about finding out who you are, what you are capable of, and what is truly possible for you.

Consciousness unlocks the trauma and drama of life.

Is now the time for you to go from dramatic to pragmatic?

Are you up for the adventure?

CHAPTER THREE

CHANGE CAN BE EASY AND FAST— NOT ONLY FOR AMERICANS

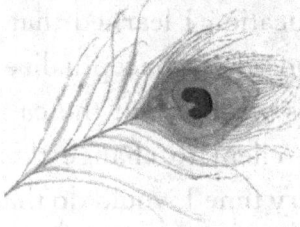

As we grow up we learn that change takes time and hard work. Easy and fast is not possible; it is supposed to be a fantasy. Europeans say that easy and fast is "so American," which is a judgment many Europeans have that Americans are doing everything quick and easy, like fast food.

Most people take pride in working hard for something, and if it is easy and fast it is not real, not valuable and only superficial. Especially as a psychologist you learn about all the ways to create change for people and how that is done and that it definitely takes time and effort.

The primary point of view in psychology is that we need to make things better for people. The goal is to get people to feel better and to get them over their problems and to make them fit in and become functional members of society. There is a certain standard to what is right and what is wrong. What is sane and what is insane. Having standards is maintaining the status quo which means leaving things as they have always been. This is what keeps the world in the same circle over and over without creating anything different. It is changing things, but it is not creating something different. It is about surviving, not thriving.

Same, same but different—start using your GPS

During my education I learned that when I work with a client I am supposed to conceptualize what the problem is, find out what is wrong, find the cause to the problem, and then help the client to change their way of thinking and behaving. Every time I would do that, my clients would come up with even more things that are wrong with them and why they are wrong. It would never stop. It is like a dragon where you cut off one head and then ten more ugly heads show up. It never changed anything. My clients and I would just feel worse and worse and we'd feel like failures for not getting anywhere. We were trapped in the matrix of this reality, making all the insanities real and making them more real by trying to understand them. It never created anything different. It just maintained the same problems.

Creating something different is not about looking at what is wrong with you and digging deep into the "wrongness" and finding the cause to your problems. How many times has that worked for you and really created something greater for you and your life? Or have you just felt even more wrong and heavy?

When you look at what is wrong and try to fix that, it requires you to judge yourself and the situation as though that is what it takes to get out of it. Judgments create more judgments and all you do is go deeper and further into judgment. People think that this is the way to create. No, judgment maintains the same old problems.

For example, in relationships people judge whether their partner did what they expected them to do in order to come to a conclusion if the relationship is good or bad. "Did they bring me flowers this week? Did they put the toilet seat down?" They judge their children if they are behaving as they are supposed to. People think that judging is the way they can make things become the way they want them to be. Except it never works. All it does is create frustration.

With conclusion and judgment that there is something wrong, nothing greater can come into your awareness than what matches the wrongness that you have decided is real.

To invite yourself to something different ask yourself:

What is right about me I am not getting?

This question will take you out of the autopilot of wrongness and start opening the doors for you to receive you.

Many times I have met clients who began acknowledging the greatness of themselves during our sessions, and then they had a doctor's appointment and they felt bad about themselves again. Why? Because the doctor was looking at them through the eyes of "here we have someone with a problem" and the focus was on the assumption that there was something wrong.

What they got out of that was more wrongness because they believed the doctor was right. When I asked them to receive the gift in that, they became aware that what the doctor says is nothing but the doctor's point of view and not real. They found out that nobody, no doctor or other expert, knows better than themselves what is actually going on. They learned to trust themselves. That is exactly what starts to open the doors to something greater: You getting out of judgment and starting to trust your awareness.

Your awareness is one of the most valuable things you have. It tells you what will make your life easier and greater. It is the GPS—the Global Possibility System—you may have not yet started using. It is so easy. Start trusting that "what is light is right"and move in that direction towards Easy Street. When things become heavy and dark you know you have to change direction towards something that is light. Power up your GPS!

This is a totally different paradigm of creating change and being in the world. So give yourself some time to open up to that new way of being. Not many people around you know about this yet. People around you make problems, judgments, thoughts and feelings real and relevant. What if they are not?

You are not your problems, your thoughts or your feelings. You are so much more. You do not have to understand why you have problems or what causes them. "What?" you may say. Yes. You know what is possible. And what is that? It is your choice to not make other's points of view and judgments real anymore, and to find out what is real for you. How? This is what I am about to tell you.

Letting go of the significance of drama and trauma allows who you truly are and what you truly would like to create to actualize in your world way easier and faster than you can imagine. Most people love drama and trauma. It is the soap opera that makes their life interesting. Most people would rather maintain their drama and trauma than be free.

Allowing yourself to be free, you get to be you. What I hear clients say is, "My whole life changed so much. I am no longer the effect of other people and judgments and how things are supposed to be. I have a sense of peace and joy in my world that is incredible. I go out in the world and receive everything and allow everything, the good and the bad, to contribute to me, my body and my life."

Did you know that even when people are upset with you, they can be a contribution to you? How? If you put down all your walls, receive what they have to say, let it go through you, and have no point of view that it can hurt or effect you. People who are angry deliver a lot of energy. If you do not see that as bad, you can receive the energy as vitalizing just by putting down your barriers. Try it. It is fun. And if you have this point of view, they do not stay angry for long.

Yes, this is new and different. What if there was nothing wrong with new and different?

Even if nobody you know has that perspective, if it is light and expansive for you, why would you not choose that just because nobody else you know is doing it? Are you willing to be the leader of your life? The worst thing that can happen is that you start to be happy, and that you might be the only happy person on your block. And even worse, that you are the invitation to others to that possibility.

The reaction trance dance

How much of your life is based on other people's points of view that you have decided you cannot go beyond? In this reality we have learned to react in certain ways to certain situations. When you lose somebody your reaction is supposed to be sad. When your boyfriend meets his ex-girlfriend you are supposed to be upset. When you are in a traffic jam you are supposed to get stressed or angry. There are certain mechanisms that we have learned that is normal to function from. It is functioning from the autopilot called this reality. Reaction never gives you choice. You are always looking for the right way to behave, fit in and be normal.

Anger, sadness, fear, pain…. Is all that real or is it an invention? What makes it real is that you make it real because everybody else does the same. Have you ever been in an extreme situation? For example, you lose somebody who was very close to you and the second you get the information you don't have a reaction? Then you start to think about the appropriate reaction, and that computation gets created in a split second and you go into other people's universes to figure out what is right in that situation and what is the appropriate way to react.

Some weeks ago my cat died. He was very, very dear to me, and was with me for many years. When he died I had no reaction at all. I was totally at peace. No sadness, no feelings, no emotions. After a couple of minutes my brain tried to compute the whole situation and tried to do what is right, which is to be sad and cry. So I cried for a while and then I asked, "What is this thing I call sadness? Is this really sadness or something else?" Since "something else" made me and my body relax, I knew that I was on the right track. Immediately, things lightened up, and I was at peace again and started laughing.I knew that what I had misapplied as sadness was joy and gratitude for my cat. How did I get so lucky to have had so many wonderful moments with him?

My cat's demise was supposed to be something that should have caused sadness and grief. That would have been the "right" reaction. Being sad would have proven how much I cared for my cat. Not being sad when someone dies is judged as being cold and not caring, or as a reaction that is suppressed and not healthy, which is just another way of saying that it is wrong.

How many times have you heard, "You do not have any feelings," meaning that you are cold and mean? Feelings are something that are used to prove a connection. By finding out what was truly going on, and that I was not sad at all when my cat died, but rather I was grateful for my cat, I acknowledged the amazing connection my cat and I had, and there was no need to prove anything anymore with feelings. I was totally aware and receiving the contribution my cat was to me and I to the cat.

Thoughts, feelings and emotions are inventions people create to make themselves "real" and right in this reality, to fit in, and to prove that they care. What if you do not have to make you "real" anymore, or fit in, or prove anything, but simply know that you are such an amazing gift?

What if you tried a different approach?

Get over giving your power to somebody or something else

You know the voices that tell you that you have a problem and that you will never get out of it? Every time you try to make your problems logical and try to find a reason for them, you make all those voices real. You give them power instead of claiming it yourself. You make those voices stronger and more valuable than yourself. They are just voices and thoughts and feelings—how can they be even remotely greater than you? Making all that greater than you maintains the status quo of your situation and allows no change. You give away all your capacities and your potency to change what is going on. You make yourself the effect of everything you make real.

All those thoughts in your head that tell you that you are not good enough, that you are bad, ugly, and that you do not know what to do, or where to go, or how to solve your problems, are inventions of your mind. They are only real if you make them so. How can you get rid of them? This is the part where it gets pragmatic!

To get rid of all those voices that tell you how terrible and wrong you are, you can say this sentence about ten times every time a thought like that whispers in your ear. Just say:

Go back to from whence you came, never to return to me or this reality.

What you do with that sentence is you send away all those voices that make you feel bad, weak and pathetic and tell you that you do not have a choice. It makes you take charge over your life and demand that everything that limits you go away.

I know it sounds weird but it totally works. (By the way. Do you know what "weird" means? It means "of spirit, of fate and of destiny." Now does it sound like fun to be weird?)

People who think they have problems put themselves in the passenger seat of their lives. Demanding change makes you take action to create what you truly desire. The sentence I shared above is designed to send away everything that tells you that you are a victim, that you do not have choice, and that your place is in the passenger seat, not in control of your life.

Try it out, what do you have to lose? Do it now! Use that sentence and say it to everything that whispers in your ear that you are weak, don't have a chance, that you will never be able to get what you truly desire, and that saying this sentence will not help.

What if you are way more powerful than you have ever acknowledged? Does that make you lighter? What is light is true for you!

Who or what do you make more powerful than yourself?

I worked with a young man with ADD and OCD who was on medication when we first met. He said that his doctor had said he needed the medication to function, otherwise his "illness" would take over and run his life. I listened to him and asked if that was also his point of view. I asked him what he knew. A week later he came back smiling with shiny eyes and said that he had "dumped" his pills.

"How can those little things be more powerful than me?" he said. "What crap I had bought from my doctor that I need them." He has not taken his medication ever since and has no problems with ADD and OCD. He was willing to receive a different perspective and the tools to use his ADD and OCD to his advantage.

This is not about telling you that you should throw away all your medications. It is an invitation for you to ask questions.

What do you know?

What does your body know?

"Body—Do you really require those pills?"

Many people never ask their bodies what they truly require. They think the doctor knows better than they do, so they take medication. The doctor prescribes the medicine based on general information on how medication works, not so much depending on how your body functions. Your body knows what it requires. It is its own expert. You can use muscle testing to find out what your body requires.

Here's how to muscle test: Stand up straight with your feet together and put the pills in front of your solar plexus and ask your body if it requires the pills now. If the body leans towards the pills, it is a yes. If it moves away from the pills, meaning backwards, it is a no. If it goes sideways, you need to ask more specific questions. "Body do you require half a pill now? Do you require one pill now? Do you require it later? Do you want to have the pill next to the bed during sleep?" Just keep on asking until you receive the awareness of what your body requires. The more you ask, the better you will be at receiving the awareness. Play with it! You can do the same with food and drinks.

Trust what you know

It is not that you lack self confidence, what you lack is trusting what you know. You are the only person who knows what is true for you. Once you start acknowledging and trusting this you will not have any more problems.

That is all it takes. Start today. Choose what makes you and your body relax, what makes you feel light, what you know is right and expands your world, and honor you enough to make that choice even if people around you disagree. What are you waiting for? Haven't you made other people's points of view more valuable than what you know long enough? What can you choose right away, right now that expands your reality? A walk, a nice meal, calling a caring person, playing with a dog, cuddling with a cat, letting go of the wrongness of you, and staying determined that your life changes no matter what?

What is it in your reality that gives you a sense of you? Write a list of what that is and do at least some of that every day. What if you are the number one priority in your life?

There are many people who say that they desire a better life and that they would like to get over their problems except many of them lie. They have no interest in getting over anything. In fact they enjoy their suffering. It took me a while to realize that. I had the illusion that once somebody tells me that they desire to change, they mean it. Oh boy, was I mistaken. I had to find out the hard way that I had to ask a question before every session. "Truth, does this person really desire to change?"

"Truth, are they interested and will they receive a different possibility?" I say "truth" before every question which allows me to know whether the person is lying or not.

Giving up your "insanity," which is what people use to define and limit themselves, takes a lot of courage. Many people would rather keep their "insanity" as it makes them feel connected to this reality. Being "insane" keeps you within the spectrum of normality. Letting go of that allows you to be totally off the scale, to be the total deviant or "freak" you truly are—outside of the confines of the status quo.

Problems: simply a matter of choice

Asking the question as to whether my clients really would like a greater life allowed me to see that many people enjoy their problems and their "insanity." It works for them. It is who they think they are and how they make their lives work. They are functional with their depression and anxieties. Once I did not have any judgments about it and did not force change upon my clients, my work became a lot easier and my clients had the choice to change or not.

Many of my clients became aware of the fact that they had no desire to get over their depression. They allowed themselves to receive that awareness and learned to not judge their choice. That created another possibility; it planted a seed that could grow into a greater reality when they chose. Becoming aware of one's choice to not change and to be depressed is such a great gift. There is nothing wrong with that. It's just a choice. Ask yourself:

Truth, do I truly desire to get over my problems?

What did you become aware of by asking that question? Let us use that awareness and ask more questions.

If you become aware that up until now you did not truly desire to change your problems, ask:

What is the value of holding on to my problems?

Is it making sure that you have people who support you? Ensuring you will have something to do? Ensuring that you will not be more than you have decided you could be? Limiting your awareness so you will not receive what you know and are truly capable of? So you will not feel too different? So your life does not get too easy? To ensure you are not too potent?

What is it for you? Whatever makes you smile or laugh, makes your body relax, or makes your world lighten up, is a hint for you to know what is true for you.

Once you realize that there is some value in maintaining your problems, you can look at them with no point of view and no judgments. What if there is nothing wrong with finding out that maintaining your problems has value to you! And maybe you can start laughing about the fact that you made all that more valuable than being you. Aren't we funny? We make all that crap more real than who we truly are. Our species is not the brightest and yet we think we are so smart.

Asking for change

When people ask for personal change, usually they ask for change out of a negative point of view. Something is "bad" and they ask for something "good." So they go from one polarity, the bad, to the other pole, the good. Both of them have charge. The one has negative charge and the other has positive charge. The thing that most people do not get is that they go from one pole to the other like a pendulum back and forth, changing from happy to sad and back and forth, except nothing different gets created.

Instead of asking for change, ask for what does not work in your life to dissipate so something different can show up. People usually ask for something positive when they feel bad. This is just maintaining yourself within the polarity, which never creates something different. You might be in a positive mode for a while and feel good and always have the "fear" that you might end up in the negative again, as though you do not have control over it. Have you ever had this constant nagging voice when you finally feel good that tells you that this won't last long? This is exactly what happens when you stay within the polarity of good and bad. It's like playing tennis, back and forth. What if you were this free space where something totally different can enter your world? Yes, it is possible. Just keep on reading.

The magic of questions. Would you like some change now?

Here are questions you can use daily to create a greater living: "What else is possible that generates and creates a totally different reality for me? How can it get any better than this?" You can ask these question every time you are looking for something greater. When you just found 10 dollars on the pavement you can ask, "How does it get any better than this?" When you have a fight with your friend, you can ask, "How does it get any better than this?" Everytime you ask, you keep on creating more rather than giving up.

With a question you open up the door for the whole universe to contribute to you, greater and beyond what you can imagine. Questions are the magic charm that take you out of what does not work, which are all the conclusions and judgments to what actually does work. Every conclusion is where you have decided there is a problem—when you keep on walking that same road, nothing will change.

For example, if you say that you have money problems and that you don't have any money you have created a conclusion, an answer that tells you that you have money problems. It is like walking in the world with blinders on and all you see is straight ahead along the road that is called Problem Street.

I have a friend who told me she had money problems and she almost could not afford rent anymore. She was very worried. Not having any money had been an answer that she had been living with for a long time. I asked her, "So what else is possible for you now, what can you be or do differently to change this?" She said, "Funny, when you ask that it makes me feel lighter and I know there is something even if I cannot put words to what it is."

The next day she told me she had continued asking this question and she suddenly remembered there was an old insurance claim that she had not gotten the money from yet.

She called the company and found out that it was time for her to receive the money, which was a large sum.

Asking questions allows you to know what you don't know when you are trapped by conclusions and judgments that something is wrong.

When you decide that something or someone is perfect, that is also a judgment and an answer that traps you. It is the answer that keeps you from accessing more. People say, "This is the perfect man, this is the perfect job...." When you have that point of view, you will not receive the information when that person is not so perfect and when being with them actually makes your life smaller. It takes you out of awareness and makes you the victim to everything you are not willing to know.

People wonder why it suddenly does not feel so good anymore to be with the person with whom it used to be so perfect. Asking everyday, "What is possible today with this person, job...that expands my life?" will give you the information you require to create what you truly desire.

Ask questions! Getting over mental illness and finding what is true

All you have to do is ask and receive. As soon as you do not make your problems, thoughts and feelings relevant and significant anymore and start asking questions, you can receive what is truly possible.

So I am asking you: Are sadness, depression and anxiety real, or are they inventions that people create? Just because you feel them does not make them real. People think that what they feel is real. You are not your feelings. Feelings are like the weather. Would a tree confuse itself with the rain? No, it knows it is just rain and something that changes and will pass by.

Would you be willing to let go of the idea that everything you feel must automatically be real? Saying, "I feel bad or depressed" is a statement that locks you up with bad feelings and depression. Nothing else that does not match that statement can enter your universe. It is like a wall that keeps out possibilities that could change the whole situation to something different with ease. You have already decided that you are sad. Does that answer make you feel lighter? What if you asked questions such as:

What is it?

What do I do with it?

Can I change it ?

How can I change it?

In deciding that you are depressed you are buying a lie. A lie is a lie and cannot be changed. The questions above can change your whole life. Are you willing?

Asking those questions opens the door to you becoming aware of what you are aware of instead of buying the answer that there is something wrong. When you ask those questions you are not looking for an answer. It is like the example of the lady with the money who asked and then became aware that there is a different possibility, even if she could not put words to what it was. She got the information about what it was later. So ask and perceive the whisper of the possibility that makes you feel lighter and allow it to show up when it shows up, when it is time.

Are you willing to have a different perspective and start asking a question whenever you "feel" sad, depressed or anything else that is "heavy?" Are you willing to give up all your conclusions and answers about how wrong, bad and sad you are, and ask yourself what you are aware of that you have never acknowledged?

How much of your sadness and depression and fear is a cover up for the potency you truly are? How much of your capacities and potency to change are you hiding underneath all the lies you have been buying about you? Does your universe lighten up when you read this? You might want to look at this and ask yourself if that is true for you.

I have a friend who suffered from migraines for over ten years. He had tried all kinds of methods known to mankind to change the migraines and nothing had worked. He had told me about his migraines many times, and one day he asked a question about it. Before that he just told me his story about how terrible it is to have such painful headaches.

The day he asked a question, for the first time he became aware of a possibility for change in his universe. He demanded something different and the question he started to ask was the door opener. He asked, "What is this thing I call migraine? Can I change it?"

I asked him,"Truth, do you really desire to change it?" He looked at me and said, "Of course I do, it is so painful, I almost wanted to kill myself, because I could not bear the pain anymore. I have tried everything and it does not work." I said, "Yes, that is the logical answer. Instead of saying what you think, tell me, what is it you know? Truth, do you really desire to get over your migraines?" and he looked at me and said, "No" and started to smile and his body relaxed.

He was so surprised by this awareness and he knew it was true as it created lightness and ease in his world and in his body. So I asked him, "What are the migraines? Is what you call migraines, really migraines or something else?" Something else made him feel lighter. So I asked, "What is it?" He started to laugh and I asked, "Is what you call migraines actually orgasms? Have you misapplied and misidentified pain with orgasm and orgasm with pain?" He looked at me with big eyes and started to laugh and laugh and laugh. I could perceive how his whole world changed. He became aware of what was true. Awareness makes you feel lighter.

The answer was not on a cognitive level or an interpretation or an analysis. It was an acknowledgment of what was really going on and what was true for him. It took him out of being a victim and into being empowered to know what he knows. It was based on what created more lightness in his world and body.

He became aware of how much joy he was suppressing and locking into his body with pain and suffering. He remembered when the migraines started, which was when his family got a residence permit in Sweden after having waited for it for a long time. He became aware that he tried hard to be like Swedes and fit in, controlling himself to not be too much, and how much of who he truly is he had cut off and suppressed so he was not being the joyful and orgasmic being he truly is.

How much intensity of you, of being and living are you hiding beneath depression, sadness, anger, fear, pain or anything you say you cannot change like money problems, or problems with relationship and body. What if you could uncover the possibilities underneath all the lies you have been buying about you and use your capacities for you and for the creation of your reality?

And what if it was way easier and faster than you could imagine?

Here it comes. Here *you* come.

CHAPTER FOUR

THE ACCESS CONSCIOUSNESS®
CLEARING STATEMENT—
BEING HARRY POTTER

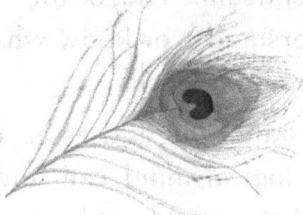

R eady for more weird? Here comes your magic wand. I told you that change can be easy and fast. It's called the Access Consciousness® clearing statement:

"Right and wrong, good and bad, pod and poc, all nine, shorts boys and beyonds.™"

The clearing statement is designed to go back to the point where you created limitations that kept you from moving forward. It allows you to clear, destroy and uncreate limitations so you have new possibilities available. It breaks down the walls that you bang your head against on a daily basis, as though it was the only choice you have; the wall you created that keeps you from being you. It changes the past so you can have a greater future.

When I heard the clearing statement for the first time, as a psychologist my mind protested wildly. I spent six years of diligent study on understanding human behavior and now I get this clearing statement, telling me I can change things so easily? I was furious. Yet I know that every time I use the clearing statement, it changes something for me. So after a while of protesting, I asked my mind to step aside and just use it. What did I have to lose? My mind? Yes! And the freedom that shows up is incredible.

To find out more about this phenomenal tool, visit www. theclearingstatement.com. The beauty is that you really don't need to understand it or know what the words mean. You can just use it and it works.

The clearing statement addresses everything that is beyond what the logical mind can understand. If every-thing was logical there would not be any problems. I found that talking about a problem, trying to understand it and analyzing it, only takes you to where the mind can go, and not beyond. This does not dissipate the problem. The clear-ing statement takes you further and clears everything that is created by the mind, and everything else that is beyond thoughts and feelings that is on an energetic level.

How to use the clearing statement

Ask a question about an area in your life that you would like to change. For example, with depression you could ask: What is the value of being depressed? That might bring up some ideas about what the value might be and it also brings up an energy: The energy of what the value is for you of being depressed. You would not be depressed if there would not be a value to it.

Notice this is not logical. If it were, you would have fig-ured out the solution already and you would not have any problems.

Asking a question allows you to access what keeps the limitations in place beyond your logical point of view. The clearing statement works on your logical point of view — and everything that is not logical — to dissipate a problem.

I worked with a lady who became aware that the value of holding on to her depression was so she could keep her husband. The depression was like a glue for her marriage. Her point of view was as long as I am depressed, I am a victim and he has to take care of me. Once I am cured he will not like me anymore and he will leave. Now that I am depressed he cannot leave me because he would feel guilty. She was not aware of that point of view before she asked the question. She thought that she wanted to get over her depression and judged herself for never getting over it. Her depression had great value, which she became aware of.

This is an example of the insanity that most people use to create their lives. All those points of view that people do not even know that they have are running their lives.

What points of view do you have that are running your life and keeping you in constant limitation? Everything that is, everything that comes up in your universe, all of it — the stuff you can put words to and the stuff that comes up energetically that you cannot put words to — will you allow yourself to let it go and destroy and uncreate it all? All you need to do is to say "yes" if you would like to let the limitations go. And now we use the clearing statement to dissipate, destroy and uncreate the limitations.

Right and wrong, good and bad, pod and poc, all nine, shorts, boys and beyonds.

The clearing statement reminds you of the potency you are and that you have what it takes to change everything you desire in your life. How? By choosing it. By saying yes and by choosing to destroy and uncreate it and open the door to a greater possibility.

Let's do it together.

What is the value of creating you as less than you truly be?

Everything that is, will you destroy and uncreate it?

Yes? Thank you.

Right and wrong, good and bad, pod and poc, all nine, shorts, boys and beyonds.

If you create problems and limitations, how much are you creating you as less than you truly are? How much of you do you have to cut off to create yourself as limited as you are pretending to be? A little, a lot or more than a lot? Running that clearing above allows you to access all the places where you are doing that in your life. You do not have to go through each and every single limitation in your life and clear them individually. The clearing statement is like a big vacuum cleaner that sucks up everything in the way of you having a clean space. The space you are. The space that allows you to choose your reality.

Another way to explain the clearing statement is with a house of cards. If you have a problem, you are building it up like a house of cards. You started at some point to create the problem and then you build it up with another layer on top, and one more, and one more. You could start examining your problem by looking at the card on the top and working your way down until you reach the bottom to find out the reasons to your problems. Examining the reasons for a problem is a lot of work that does not lead anywhere besides deeper into the problem. It does not change it.

I like fast and efficient. As a psychologist you are not supposed to have that point of view. It is supposed to be my job to work through my clients' problems. Work has never been my best talent and ability. I like to play and I enjoy changing things with ease, and creating different possibil- ites. The clearing statement is more my style: Quick, easy and without side effects.

The only thing required is choice. The choice to let go of the limitations you have created. How does it get any better than that? It reminds you of the fact that you are the one who can change it, that you have everything it takes to do that, and that you can change it now. One more time:

What is the value of creating you as less than you truly be?

Everything that is, will you destroy and uncreate it? Yes?

Right and wrong, good and bad, pod and poc, all nine, shorts, boys and beyonds.

Keep on running that process to open up the doors to being more of You.

The clearing statement clears what you use to separate you from what is truly possible for you. It gets you out of your mind and into question. Questions that open up new possibilities. Your mind gives you answers that keep you in the hamster wheel of the same old over and over. It's all the thoughts, feelings, emotions, computations, judgments and conclusions about what you should do and should not do, what is right and what is wrong that maintain limitations. It keeps you in a constant state of thinking and doing and calculating. All of that has an electrical charge and keeps you within polarity.

Being beyond polarity allows you to access the space of you where you get to choose what you would like to create as your life which can be different in every moment. Using the clearing statement facilitates you to access all that as it dissipates the positive and the negative charge in every area of your life.

What else is possible? The question, choice, possibility and contribution that generate the forward movement of your life. When you ask the questions that open up doors to greatness, you can go beyond what you could ever imagine and the whole universe contributes to you.

I use the clearing statement when I become aware of a limitation that I am choosing to let go of, and I use it with my clients.

CHAPTER FIVE

THOUGHTS, FEELINGS AND EMOTIONS TO BE NORMAL

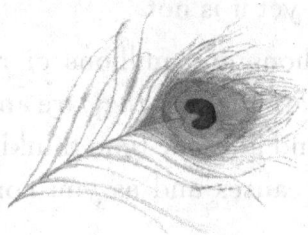

The way people define themselves is through who they think they are, which means they define themselves and their world by thinking and by feeling. Thinking, feeling and emoting has great value in this reality, especially in psychology. The point of view is that in order to change anything, one must understand what is going on (which is thinking) and one must feel and emote.

"Understanding" means standing under, which is exactly what you do when you try to understand something or someone. You are making yourself stand under the thing or person to try to get why something or someone is the way they are. That way, you make yourself less, you cut off your awareness and your knowing to put what is going on in the small box of thinking in order for you to understand.

The question is, what is the value of understanding? Does it solve anything? Does it really change anything? Or do you just exercise your brain until you think you have come to some kind of conclusion? You know how it is when you are trying to understand something and you think and you think and it just gets heavier and heavier. It does not change or give any clarity about what is going on. The result is frustration. Thinking is an attempt to change something, yet all it does is make you go further down the rabbit hole to find a conclusion that is supposed to somehow be satisfying, yet it is not.

There are millions and millions of reasons as to why things and people are the way they are and act the way they do. You could spend all your time thinking and coming up with reasons and causes and as you come up with more, more get created.

Thoughts, feelings and emotions are inventions and not a reality unless you make them real. Yet people are suffering every day based on their thoughts, feelings and emotions. They have solidified their own inventions into existence, finding stories to back them up.

Every time you tell yourself that you are sad, you have decided that you are sad, and then you come up with all kinds of reasons why you are sad. People are very creative when it comes to that. "Ah, my neighbors just looked at me funny, I am sure he does not like me, and by the way my dog just looked at me funny too. I know why nobody likes me, I am such a bad person...."

Thinking, feeling and emoting, sex and no sex is how you make yourself fit into this reality. Thinking is used to come to conclusion, to figure out what the right choice is. It is where you are in constant judgment and constant deciding, concluding and computing. It is using you as a calculating machine to navigate through this reality to do everything right and to not make any mistakes and to win and to make sure you do not lose.

Feeling is how you turn everything you are aware of, everything you are perceiving, into something that must have something to do with you. You take an awareness and buy it as yours and conclude that it has relevance for you and that it matters.

Emotions are used to prove that you are a real human being. Emotions are many times a proving that you care instead of acknowledging that you already care and do not have to prove your caring.

Sex and no sex are the only ways in this reality people allow themselves to receive. They say, "This is a person I will have sex with," which means that this is a person they will receive from. "This person is such a loser, I would never have sex with this person," means that they are cutting off their receiving from that person, and every other person who is similar to that person.

What is beyond thinking, feeling, emoting, sex and no sex?

Being, knowing, perceiving and receiving.

The space where you get to be you, to know everything, to perceive and to receive everything without holding onto it and without having a point of view.

Welcome to a different world. Welcome to *you*.

This is where you have total freedom and are no longer the effect of the polarity of this world. To think, feel, emote, sex and no sex requires you to be finite and to contract to fit into this reality and to make what is normal and what is good and what is considered bad, real. Being, knowing and perceiving is where you are the infinite, expansive being you truly are. *This is being the space where everything is possible.*

It sounds so utopian, and you know what? I have discovered that it is possible and that it is way easier to be space than one could imagine. Being, knowing, perceiving and receiving makes functioning in this reality way easier and you get to go beyond this reality also. The door is opening for you right now. Are you walking through it, into the freedom of being you?

When I invite people to this different possibility to be, know, perceive and receive, they tell me many times that this is not possible, that one must think and feel to function, and that it is necessary to think and feel to get by in life, and to do what is required on a daily basis, like work.

When I was in Australia at a seven-day intense Access Consciousness® class, it opened up the doors to be the space I truly am. There were no thoughts, feelings or emotions in my head, just ease and joy. I went to the airport to depart from Australia and I was handed this form I should fill out with all kinds of information about myself. I remembered my name, which was great, then they asked for some other information, which I could find in my passport, and then they asked for the date. I usually do not know the date, so I just looked at my iPhone. Then they asked for the year. Well, again I checked my iPhone, only to find out that there was nowhere it said what year it was. So I stood there and started laughing at the fun of not knowing what year it was, realizing that it does not matter.

When I do psychological testing, one of the questions in neuropsychological surveys is to ask the client what year it is to find out more about the patient's cognitive capacities.

And here I was at the airport, totally failing the test and having a great time with it. So I asked, "What else is possible?" I knew I could ask someone, "Excuse me, what year is this?" I probably would have earned a pitiful look. So I asked again, "What else is possible?" and then one more question, "Universe, please help me out here, I am having a not so bright moment here, what year do we have? What do people call this year?" Immediately the number 2010 came to my awareness. The funny thing was I could not verify in my brain whether that number was right or wrong, but I knew without a doubt that it was correct. And it was. That was when I got the difference between thinking and knowing. And that I can just ask for the information I require and I know.

Knowing is much faster and lighter than thinking, which takes time. Thinking is based on the judgments, on the polarity of right or wrong. Knowing is receiving information without a point of view.

This is how I book my plane tickets and make hotel reservations and all other things that are part of this reality. I ask, "What hotel is fun and ease to stay at? What hotel makes my life easier?" And then I know without having to figure it out or compare hotels.

A while ago I booked a hotel in Costa Rica, and when I got there, some locals asked me how come I chose this hotel. I wondered why they were asking me. They said because it is the best hotel on the whole beach and almost nobody seems to know about it. The price is great and it has the most beautiful beachfront. They asked how I possibly could find it. Easy: by asking and trusting my knowing.

I could have gone on the Internet, looked at hotels and compared them, and worked hard to find something which

I think is good. What I did was ask a question and follow my knowing. Knowing is sensing what is light and expands your universe. Thinking takes time and has more charge, and if you do a lot of it, it gives you a headache.

Being, knowing, perceiving and receiving is possible for all of us when we let go of the necessity of thinking, feeling and emoting.

The pragmatic way of looking at this is by asking the questions: Is thinking, feeling and emoting *real*? Is it getting you where you would like to go? Is it giving you the freedom you desire? In other words, does it really work for you? And is there an alternative you could choose where thinking, feeling and emoting is a choice and not a necessity to live in this reality?

When I watch movies like *Avatar* I cry. I enjoy the feelings and emotions that come up and the awareness and the joyful knowing of a greater possibility. It is all included. Nothing is judged. The feelings are a choice and I enjoy them. I do not have the point of view that feelings are a necessity. They are an invention. Most people just buy them as real and not many ask questions about them. They just assume that feeling, especially feeling bad, is part of the deal of being on this planet and that it's natural.

What if it is not? Have you ever asked yourself what else is possible? Have you somehow always known that being you and being on this planet could somehow be way easier and more joyful? Yes it can. How? Easy: Choose it. Allow yourself to be the difference you truly are, the controversy, the deviation from the norm. What do you have to lose? What you are capable of is changing the world. Your world.

How to access being, knowing, perceiving and receiving

Here are tools for you:

Who does this belong to?

What is light is right, what is heavy is a lie.

The majority of your thoughts, feelings and emotions are not yours. Does that make you feel lighter? Ask your body. Did you just relax a little bit more? The majority of what you think and feel is not yours. Most of the problems you try to handle on a daily basis are not yours. You are simply aware of the points of view, the thoughts, feelings and emotions that are going on in the world at all times. When you meet somebody who is sad, you know that they are sad without them ever telling you. You perceive their sadness. What most people do when they perceive sadness, is conclude that it is theirs and they say, "I am so sad." Just because you are aware of it and perceive it, does not mean it is yours.

So what is possible with that information? When there is any kind of heaviness in your world, a feeling, an emotion or a thought, stop and ask, "Who does this belong to?" When the heaviness, the thought, or the feeling goes away, you will see they are not yours, you were simply perceiving them. If it does not go away, you can ask yourself, "Truth, did I buy this as mine?" If you get a "yes," you'll know that you are holding on to it. You now have the choice to keep holding on, or to let go. How? Just let go.

What is the value of buying thoughts, feelings and emotions as yours? Many people conclude that just because they are aware of them that they have to do something. Many times there is nothing to be done. Just receive the awareness and allow yourself to enjoy it no matter what it is. Ask, "Can I change it?"

John Lennon was correct. If you can't change it, let it be.

Many people try to take care of others by taking on their thoughts, feelings, pain and suffering. They take all that into their bodies as an attempt to heal the other person. Sometimes it works for a while. The other person may feel better, but if they are not interested in letting go of their problem, they will soon create a new problem. And then you are both suffering.

I had a couple of clients where the child was taking care of their parents' suffering and the parents were not willing to let go of their pain. So the child was feeling the parents' pain and feeling like a failure for not succeeding to heal his or her parents. I've also had families where both the children took on their parents' suffering, and the parents took on their children's suffering, and the whole family just felt bad and had no idea why. When we accessed their awareness about that, they changed what was going on and their whole family changed.

How do you know if it is yours or not?

What makes you feel light is right, what is heavy is a lie. That is a great key to the freedom that you always knew was possible and never knew how to access. What we have learned and the way people function in this reality is that if it is heavy and solid it must be right. "It must be right" is a conclusion. What is heavy and solid and dense such as suffering and pain, "must be" real. Is that really so? What do you know?

What is light and what makes your body relax, your heart sing, and expands your life, is actually what is true for you. Everything else is inventions, lies and things others make real.

What would you like your life to be like? Get the energy of that. Is it heavy and dense or light and easy? Most likely, it will be light if you want joy and ease. To create this life, simply choose what matches that energy. Choose what is light. If you have two people who would like to go on a date with you, or if you are choosing what food to eat, or what profession to pursue, choose the one that most matches the energy you would like your life to be like. You can use this for any choice, such as movies, friends, food, living situations and so forth. Choosing what matches the energy of your reality is where every choice you make contributes to what you are creating. This is where you start creating your life, instead of simply surviving in this reality.

Being aware and conscious is where you receive everything and judge nothing. Receiving everything means not having any barriers up to the information around you. It's when you are letting the information go through you, and being the question of what is possible with what you are aware of. Every awareness can be the starting point to a greater possibility.

Most people think that if they would be totally aware of everything, that it would be too much; they would be overwhelmed and they would have to protect themselves from too much information. Let me ask you: Is that true, or does protecting yourself by putting barriers up take a lot of energy? And is there anything you have to protect yourself from?

People say there is good and bad energy. No, there is only energy. It is when you judge what you are aware of and judge the energy as bad that you decide that it will hurt you. And guess what, your point of view creates your reality; reality does not create your point of view.

Instead of being totally aware, most people would rather stay in their minds and brains so that they do not have to know what they know. They both torture and entertain themselves with their mental movies that they cannot access and receive what their bodies are aware of.

I recently had a client, a young man who very much enjoys and is tortured by his mental masturbation. He tries to make sense of the world, which does not make sense to him at all, and never has. He tries to figure out why people do what they do, and say what they do, and he tracks their reactions to him. He has Asperger's, but you do not have to have Asperger's for this to apply to you.

He never learned how to deal with everything he knows and is aware of, so his way of handling that is by going into his brain and creating his own world. It works for him. But it requires a lot of energy to keep that mind machine going and to make sure that this private place is being maintained.

He has cut off his awareness of his body. Bodies are sensory organs that pick up information of the world all the time. Staying in his brain, he created a separation where he cannot enjoy his body. He says that he is on neutral all the time and has no joy. Having no connection to your body cuts off all your receiving of everything and everyone around you, including yourself. It is like wanting to fill your cup with a delicious drink, which refreshes you and vitalizes you, but you locked the door to the fridge. Every single molecule is there to contribute to you and your body. Cutting off that connection in favor of being secure and not disturbed all by yourself in your brain keeps you from all the pleasures, possibilities and creative energies that are available for you.

Receiving what you are aware of creates a totally different playground for you.

What if your awareness was not a judgeable offense? What if it were not good nor bad, just information you can use the way you desire? This would mean more freedom for you.

A great example is Forrest Gump. Nothing brings that man down. He could be in the middle of a war and receive everything with no point of view. He receives everything and uses it to create his reality. Whatever he does, he does it from gentleness and kindness. There is no judgment in his world. No need to prove anything. And nothing is significant to him. Things change and he allows them to change without holding on to anything. No form, no structure and no significance. Being the way he is gets him further than any other person. What a smart man!

What if awareness and consciousness is the new smart?

Life is like a box of chocolate.... We do not know how it shows up but we can choose that it shows up.

CHAPTER SIX

JUDGMENTS—THE DEAD END

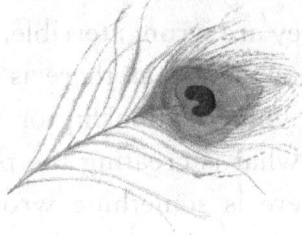

J udgments are what people use to create their lives. It is how people figure out whether what they are looking at and choosing is right or wrong, good or bad, and whether they like it or not. Most people see the world only through the filter of their judgments.

A while ago I was at an opera in Vienna and the music was flowing through my body, vitalizing every cell. The tenor was expanding the audience's worlds with his voice. In the break I was just so happy and grateful for the music and the singers. While ordering a glass of wine, I overheard a conversation with a woman who said, "Well, his singing was okay today, but I heard that he did not hit all the notes he should have." Her friend agreed and they went on judging. Wow. Really? In the presence of that beauty, these people chose to judge and cut off their possibility to receive the contribution the tenor's voice and the music was to their lives and their bodies. What unkindness to themselves.

Every time you judge, you cut off what is available for you to receive. Everything that does not match your judgment cannot come into your world.

The people I work with are in constant judgment of themselves. Every time they look at themselves, they look through the eyes of judgment. They've made decisions and conclusions that they are wrong, terrible, worthless or ugly. Having the point of view that there is something wrong with your body or your relationship or your money situation or yourself is what is creating the problem. It is your conclusion that there is something wrong that leaves no room for anything else to be created or to come into your world.

Wrongness in all shapes and forms, usually justified by, "In the past, this and this happened, my childhood was this and that," is the story that people use to explain, reason and justify why they have the problems they have, why they cannot change it, and why their life is so hard.

I never listen to, tell or buy the story. When clients say, "This and that is my problem, because..." they are beginning the story. Everything that comes after "because" justifies why they have a problem, why they are right to have the problem, and why they cannot change what they say they would like to change. That is leaving them in maintaining the circle of their problem. Listening to and buying people's stories is telling them they are right for keeping their story, and that they are indeed the victims of their own story.

What else is possible?

Asking questions empowers people by not buying their stories and not seeing them as victims. It invites them to the awareness that they have what it takes to change what they desire to change.

When my clients realize their reasons and justifications for why they have problems are simply stories that they have created, and that their stories are not real or fixed, they lighten up as they realize they can open up the door to an entirely new reality of their choosing.

Every story is just an interesting point of view. You can look at it that way or this way, and depending on the mood you are in and who you talk to, your story changes. Your past is what you judge it to be. There is nothing fixed about it. It is your judgments about your story that determines how you calculate what is probable for you in the future. It is creating your future based on your past, which does not leave you a lot of choice. You choose from the menu of your past.

What about letting your past be an interesting point of view instead of a fixed point of view? What about letting your past be non-significant and allow it to be what you chose to be and do before this moment? What about allowing yourself to choose being who you are right now? How many more choices would you have available? Your menu just increased dramatically, no?

Many people were not acknowledged for their brilliance when they were children. They were mostly judged for not being good enough. What if you treated yourself the way you would like to have been treated, instead of suffering for the way you were treated? Wouldn't that change your future?

Stories can be fun when they expand your world and inspire you, not if you use them to justify your limitations.

I was working with a woman who was sexually abused when she was a teenager. We were talking about the abuse and she said that she no longer wished to be limited by her past. She had used the abuse to justify that she cannot enjoy her life any longer and that she hates her body. When she became aware of that, she was ready to let go of justifying her limitations, and that opened up the door to where she could receive my facilitation to change what the abuse created in her world and her body. By addressing what got created by the abuse, the energy that was stuck in her body could be released.

In her session a week later, she had a big smile and she said that so much had changed for her. She now enjoys her body, and it is like the abuse never happened. It is not relevant anymore. She changed her past. She is a different person now and knows she can choose whatever she desires.

What are you choosing?

Are you willing to stop judging yourself?

How much are you trying to prove that you are good enough and not wrong by proving to yourself and others how smart you are? Proving that you are smart requires constant judgments of yourself. You are in constant surveillance of yourself to figure out whether you are smart enough or not. All that gets accomplished is a smoking head.

Another judgment that people use is proving how dumb they are over and over to not know how smart they truly are.

Everybody has their own way of judging themselves out of the capacities they truly have available. Being the greatness you are would require you to be in total allowance of yourself. Total allowance is where you receive everything and judge nothing. It is where you no longer need to hide anything from yourself and others with the point of view that any part of you is too ugly for others to see. Every ugliness becomes an interesting point of view. It is not real anymore. Just an interesting point of view.

Let's play with that tool. Take something that you consider wrong, terrible and ugly about yourself. Now say to that point of view, "It's an interesting point of view that I have this point of view." Now look at the point of view again as it is now and say again, "Interesting point of view, I have this point of view," and perceive how it is now...and say it again, "Interesting point of view I have this point of view." Now look at your point of view again. Is it changing?

For points of view and judgments you've had of yourself for a long time, you might have to do this 20 times or more. Do it until it lightens up or you start to relax. Some people start laughing when they do this as they realize how funny it is to have the points of view they have and how relaxing it is to let go of them.

You can use this tool for everything that "feels" heavy. You can use it for your points of view and for other people's points of view. For example, if someone says that you did something wrong or are not good enough, then say in your head, "Interesting point of view, that (s)he has this point of view," until you realize that what they say is nothing but a point of view and not a reality.

I had a client whose wife was accusing him of all kinds of things. Whatever he did, it was wrong. He felt terrible and had the point of view that all the problems they had in their marriage were his fault. He tried everything to make it right for his wife. I showed him the tool of "interesting point of view" and he used it every time his wife would judge him. He lowered all his barriers and he would say in his head, "Interesting point of view that she has this point of view" (not in a sarcastic way) until he no longer made her point of view real. He could receive what she had to say, which made her lectures to him much shorter than they used to be as she felt received and had no need to prove the rightness of her point of view.

When all the points of view in the world are nothing other than an interesting point of view, the significance of judgments get taken away. They are no longer relevant. They are just what people use to make themselves real and to fit in. Allowing yourself to be different and not trying to change yourself so you fit other people's judgments opens up the door to choice. You can receive everything and everyone as an interesting point of view and as information you can use to create your life. This is where living becomes pragmatic instead of complicated.

Choice is where you can change direction in every moment. If you have just been upset with someone, you can choose again. Would you like to continue being upset or would you like to go and have a walk in the park instead? What if no choice has to last longer than ten seconds? You are upset for ten seconds, ten seconds are over and you can choose something different.

For example, say you have just yelled at your kids and feel terrible about it. Instead of feeling bad, you could receive the choice you just made without a judgment and say to your kids, "I am sorry, I have just been a rotten parent. Please forgive me." And move on. Those ten seconds of choosing to yell are over. You have not harmed your kids with it. You have just shown them that you can sometimes make choices that are not so expansive, and that there is no need to judge those choices, and that there is always the possibility to move on and choose again. Not feeling bad about yourself is the greatest gift you can be to your kids to inspire them to not judge themselves in the future for the choices they make.

True creation does not come from judgment about what is right or wrong, but from asking questions and choosing and choosing again. Choice creates awareness.

Many people misidentify judgment with awareness. The difference between an awareness and a judgment is the energy. A judgment has a charge; it is either positive or negative. An awareness does not have a charge; it is light. Awareness makes you feel light. Judgments are heavy.

For example, if you think someone is being mean, ask if this is a judgment or an awareness. Even acknowledging someone's meanness is light when it is an awareness. The great part about this is you can use your awareness as information and know that this person might not be someone you would like to have dinner with. Consciousness includes everything and judges nothing, even meanness.

One day when I was getting ready for work, I had this knowing to stay at home and I did not know why. The day after I heard there was a man with a gun at the office threatening the staff. Reflecting back, the awareness to not go to work that day was light and had no charge even though it was about a threat. Trusting my knowing and not judging myself for being wrong to not go to work that day definitely made my life easier.

Inventions of the mind

Every upset you have is something you feed energy to and make real. You use your energy, time and creativity to make your upsets real and to find evidence for them to be bigger than your capacity to change them. Scan through your day to find out how many upsets you have had in only one day, with your family, your children, your colleagues, yourself, your body, your money, your business…. Every time something lacks ease, which is your natural being, you are creating an upset and making it real.

What a great and glorious inventor you are; inventing your upsets every day in every moment just to be normal and real like everybody else. What if you could use your capacity for invention and creativity to your advantage and create something that actually works for you?

How many of your upsets are inventions that are actually awarenesses that you have not acknowledged and twisted into judgments which are creating the troubles in your life? If you did not understand a word of what you just read, that is totally appropriate. Just laugh and nod. That is what we foreigners do when we don't understand and just want to be polite.

Not understanding is exactly where we would like to get. This is the point where you no longer create from the limitations of your mind and open up to your knowing, which sometimes seems like suddenly not getting anything anymore. Enjoy the nodding. Reading or hearing something like this and not getting it may just let you know that this is your item. When it is your item, your brain does not get it anymore as it goes beyond its capacity to figure it out. This is the point where you can go beyond your limitations. Don't worry, be happy and grateful and just keep on reading.

For example, when you are aware of someone stealing from you, you have just received information that you could use to your advantage. Ask yourself what you would like to choose that would make your life easier. Would you like to talk to the person, or just let it be, or what else could you choose that expands your life? Receiving this awareness lets you know that you have choice.

If you would have the awareness that someone is stealing from you but you judge yourself by saying, "I must be wrong, what a terrible thought, this person would never steal from me...." you have just twisted an awareness into a thought and a judgment and created an invention which creates an upset in your reality.

Let's put the clearing statement into action to change that!

How much of your awareness are you twisting into thoughts, feelings and emotions?

Everything that came up asking that question, will you destroy and uncreate it?

Right and wrong, good and bad, pod and poc, all nine, shorts, boys and beyonds.

I highly recommend running that clearing many times to access your awareness and unlock yourself from everything you have made real that is not real. By running that clearing I mean say that sentence out loud or in your head. If you run the clearing for yourself, just replace the "you" in the sentence with "I."

The next thing is defending the invention. Once you invent something, you defend it. For example, if you invented the point of view that nobody likes you, then you will defend that invention by looking for evidence that nobody likes you. You will project onto other people that they do not like you, you will study their faces to find signs they don't like you, you will put in their heads that they don't like you, which they will prove to you by avoiding you or being mean to you.

Can you see how that works? It is insane. And everything is just an invention.

How can you change it?

By being aware of it. By becoming more and more aware that the upset in your life is just an invention; choosing to let it go is all it takes to change it.

To make it even easier, you can run this process over and over again:

What invention am I using to create the upset I am choosing?

Everything that is, will you destroy and uncreate it?

Right and wrong, good and bad, pod and poc, all nine, shorts, boys and beyonds.

CHAPTER SEVEN

SYMPTOMS INTO DIAGNOSIS AND WHERE ARE YOU?

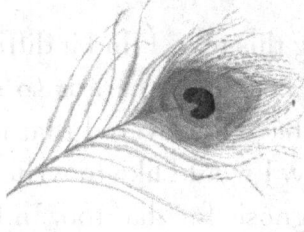

Summarizing symptoms into categories called diagnoses is one of the main ways of creating order in the area of mental health. People are so complex in their ways of thinking and behaving that it creates chaos and a need to create order. There are so many rules on how to behave and what is right and what is wrong, that many people feel lost and desperately do everything they can to get it right to be accepted and to fit in.

The diagnosis system is reference points to judge what is normal and right and what is not normal. It is a creation that changes every year and is designed to make sense out of something that actually does not make sense. Most people feel "wrong" and then get evidence of how wrong and sick they are when they have a diagnosis. Others use it as reason and justification that they are incapable of creating their lives. Changing that and letting go of one's reference points and definitions of self takes a lot of courage.

Diagnosing has never really assisted me in my work. I recognize how every patient is different. One person can fit into many diagnoses at the same time or into none of them. The times when I consulted my diagnosis book and finally found a matching diagnosis I have never been sure what I really have accomplished. I have categorized a person's symptoms. Alright. And now? What to do with this information?

As I am writing this text, I find it difficult to write about one subject at a time. Since there is so much I would like to say, so much I have discovered that is so different than current psychology, I would like to write it all at once. I am sure there is a diagnosis for that too. In fact, I am ADHD, ADD, autistic and OCD all at the same time, and a psychologist, and on top of that I look totally normal (whatever that is).

Notice that I said I "am" ADHD…. There is a difference between having a diagnosis and *being*. Having a diagnosis is having symptoms that can be summarized into a specific category. Those are written in books that can be found on every psychiatrist's bookshelf. They are merely inventions. Being ADHD is to have the capacities that these so called diagnoses hide. Yes, that is correct, I used the word "capacities". Later on in the book I will explore with you what those capacities are.

I have been to many lectures and read many books that refer to ADHD, ADD, autism and other mental diagnoses as disorders or deficits. Do these people really have "handicaps?" Or are they just different? If we look closer, we can perceive and receive the possibilities.

What do you know that you have not allowed yourself to know? If you go beyond what is right and real in this reality and what you have been entrained to believe, what do you truly know is possible for you and the world?

People who have been diagnosed often use those labels to describe who they are. They create themselves according to the symptoms that are summarized by "their" diagnosis and with that, validate other people's realities about how they are supposed to be. They make that picture of who they are based on the limitation of the diagnosis. I have seen this with so many patients in mental health. With the label "depression," they became even more depressed as they then had a reason and justification for being depressed.

Even theories work like diagnoses. They are structures and answers that tell you what is right and what is wrong and what road to take. You take your life and make it fit into the theory to explain it and understand it. You use it as a reference point to find the solution. But in the solution lies the trap. You use an answer to explain the life which is disempowering you.

An answer disempowers.

A question empowers.

How can a theory or diagnosis know more about you than you know about yourself?

I invite you to know what you know instead of looking at other people's points of view as more valuable than your knowing. What if you could be who you be rather than trying to fit into the box the diagnosis calls this reality?

CHAPTER EIGHT

THE SPACE CALLED YOU—
IT IS WEIRD, IT IS WACKY,
BUT IT WORKS

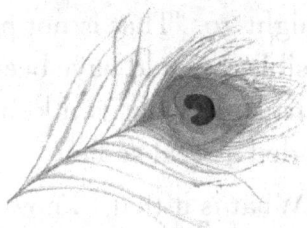

H ow much more difficult are you making your life
than it has to be? How much of your so-called
problems are you holding onto because this is
what one does in this reality? You have to have a problem
in order to be real. Everybody has one, so why should you
not have one too? Who would you be without one or two?
Have you decided that you would be too different, too
weird, if you would not create a handicap that makes you
as limited as everybody else? Life is like golf. It's all about
handicaps. Really? Is this *really* your reality?

What are you making real that is not?

Remember: What makes you light is right, what makes
you heavy is a lie. A tool you can use for everything. When
you would like to know if something is an invention and
not real, perceive the energy of it. If it is light it is an awareness you are having. If it is heavy it is a lie; someone else's
perception or point of view.

So now look through your life and perceive all the places where you are creating heaviness and ask, is this real or is all of this a lie I have been buying? Notice that your universe lightens up. This information is usually not used because in this reality it is more valuable to have problems, to make them real and to find out why one has problems rather than ask a question to change it right away. All you need to do is ask a question and turn on the lights of awareness to know what is required in order to change it. It is so easy that you might go, "That is not possible, that is too easy, if it were possible, I would have been told this before." What if you start trusting what you know instead of what you have been handed as real so far?

Ask yourself: "What is it that I know here?"

When something is right for you, you just know it beyond doubt. There is no need to use your brain to figure anything out or try to find evidence. You just know. The point of view that it cannot be that easy; does that make you lighter or heavier? Lighter means that it makes you feel more relaxed, like taking a breath. It is when you know that it is true for you, not from a cognitive point of view but from a knowing that is bigger than what you can think in your head.

So what else is in your head that makes you feel heavy? How much of what is going on in your head on a daily basis makes you feel heavy? How many of the thoughts in your head are on autopilot, going on and on without you being able to stop them, driving you crazy? Would you like to change that? Would you like to find out who you truly are beyond all that buzz in your head?

Here it comes, the information that you should have been given a long time ago: 99% of all your thoughts, feelings and emotions *do not belong to you.* They are not yours. All of them are information you are picking up from other people and the Earth. I told you that this is weird. Changing and being more of who you are requires you to let go of what has not worked so far and open the doors to something different that might be weird and a totally different world but that actually gives you the freedom of you. Trying to stop the thoughts in your head does not work; there is no "off" button. Trying to relax with all those thoughts in your head does not work either.

How many techniques have you tried that have not worked? Why do they not work? Most of those techniques agree and align with the idea that these thoughts are real and that they are yours. Everything you agree with and align to makes it real and it sticks to you. Everything you agree with and align to and resist and react to, you make real and you become the effect of it. Same with all your thoughts and feelings.

Look at the ocean. No matter whether it rains or snows or the sun shines, the ocean always is and is being with whatever storm comes up. The same with the trees. The trees are being the peace they are no matter what kind of weather meets them. They are not confusing the weather, the storm, the rain, the snow, the sun with who they are.

People always confuse their feelings (their weathers) with who they are. They say, I am sad, I am angry. This is like the tree saying, "I am the snow, I am the rain." What if you could be aware of the space you are, the peace you are, and every time you are aware of a feeling or a thought ask, "Who does this belong to?" I will say it again: 99% of your thoughts and feelings are information you pick up from other people and the Earth. Yes. You are an awareness machine of great magnitude. If you would acknowledge that, it would make your life so much easier. It would eliminate 99% of what is going on in your head.

But don't do it. You would be as peaceful as the trees and the ocean. You would be so different that others would ask you what is wrong because you would no longer get upset as you used to do. Being peaceful is a "wrongness" in this reality. Being joyful is also a "wrongness" in this reality.

I had a patient who was bipolar and she had some sessions with me, and after that she met her doctor who looked confused and said that she no longer met the criteria of being bipolar and that should be impossible; you are not supposed to be able to get rid of that diagnosis so easily. She told him how happy she is now and how joyful her life is and he asked her, "Are you on drugs?" Interesting how things are here.

So what would you like to choose? Going around and buying other people's thoughts and feelings as yours, or asking, "Who does this belong to?" Asking that question every time you "feel" heavy without having to analyze what is going on when it is not yours, it lightens up your world and allows you to perceive the space that you are. It takes practice. Do it for every thought and feeling you have for three days. At the end of those three days, you will be a walking, talking meditation. You will start out doing it and then you will forget and then you will remember it again. Don't worry. Just do it as often as you remember it. You will be surprised about how many things you thought were your problems that have nothing to do with you.

A patient with ADHD came to me because he was troubled with anxiety and social phobia and he told me how hard it is to be around other people because he gets anxious. So I asked him how much of all those other people's thoughts, feelings and emotions he was picking up and thinking that they were his. He looked at me with bright eyes and said, "This totally makes sense, it feels so true, even if it does not make logical sense. It's like I have been doing this my whole life. Feeling bad non-stop. Whatever I tried, I could not change it. That is such amazing information. I feel like me when we talk about this."

"Yes, because you are that space, that is your natural being, everything else is inventions you are aware of. They are lies and things that are not yours that you cannot change," I replied.

"It's like my whole life is changing right now when we talk about this. I thought that I was sick and mentally ill, and wow, turns out I am not."

You are also highly aware of what is going on with the Earth. You might have noticed all the changes that are going on in the world as far as the Earth is concerned. Changes in climate and weather. Ask yourself, "How much are my body and I aware of what is going on with the Earth?" How much did that lighten up your universe? You and your body and the Earth are connected. When the weather shifts, how many times has your body been aware that the weather is about to change? Whether it is psychological weather or weather outside in nature, you and your body are aware of what is going on.

You and your body are also aware of what the Earth requires of you. When you have pain in your body, ask if the Earth requires something from you.

I was working with a woman who said that she had an anger issue she would like to get rid of. One of the things that came up during our sessions was the awareness that she had stored massive amounts of energy in her body which she had misapplied and misidentified as anger she had to suppress. When we asked the question, "What does the Earth require of you?" everything immediately became lighter. I asked her to put up her hands and gather all the energy the Earth required of her and her body, and by flicking her hands send that energy to the Earth. She did that about 20 times and was totally peaceful afterward. She realized that she is space and peace. Her anger was merely the Earth asking her for a contribution that she had refused to listen to.

When you are in a room where people have been fighting and you enter the room, without having been given the information that people have been fighting, you know that something has been going on there, you know that something just happened there. Why? Because you are aware of the energy around you all the time!

The point in asking, "Who does this belong to?" is that you no longer have to buy what is not yours. You no longer have to carry the burden that has never been yours and you can be free and start creating your life the way you really would like to.

This is a tool I teach my clients all the time and those who choose to use it report how surprised they are about how many of their problems were not theirs, and how much of the problems of others they were trying to take care of by locking them into their head and body.

How much are you trying to heal others by taking on their thoughts and feelings and pain and suffering? Is that working for you? Or does it always end by you feeling bad and the other person creating new pain and suffering?

What creation of pain and suffering are you using to validate other people's realities and invalidate your reality are you choosing?

Everything that is, will you destroy and uncreate it?

Right and wrong, good and bad, pod and poc, all nine, shorts, boys and beyonds.

Every time you choose pain and suffering you validate this reality and invalidate your reality! Isn't now the time to start choosing you?

CHAPTER NINE

DISTRACTIONS—ANGER AND GUILT

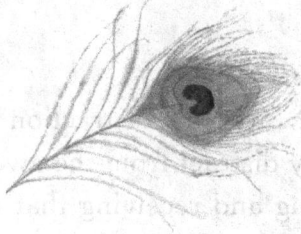

nger and guilt are distractor implants. They keep
you trapped and tell you that you do not have any
choice. They are the things that people never ask
any questions about. They assume that this is the way life
is and supposed to be. Most people agree and align to the
fact that anger is real and that guilt is real and they spend
lots of time trying to handle it. They never ask are anger
and guilt real?

Trying to handle or working hard to manage these does
not work since they are not real. What is not real and what
is a lie you cannot change. Implants are everything you
agree and align with and resist and react to which contributes to your energy to make it real. For example, if you
and I take a walk and I say, "Look at that person, look at
his face, he is so angry." (When all the person is doing, is
getting ready to sneeze.) By agreeing to my point of view
and saying, "Yes, you are right he is so angry" you have just

been implanted with a point of view. We have just invented something that is not real.

Distractor implants seem to be the problem but they are not. Many people have the point of view that anger is the problem, and so they try to talk themselves and others out of it. How well does that work?

Why distractor implants?

These implants are the distraction of what is actually going on. They distract from the awareness, the being, knowing, perceiving and receiving that is possible. Trying to handle or solve a problem or an issue you have decided you have, for example guilt, is not done by addressing the guilt and handling the guilt. How many times has that worked for you? And how much does the guilt stay or come back over and over again. It is like looking for a key in Sweden when you lost it in Germany. You will never find it in Sweden, even though you spent years and years looking for it.

Distractor implants are the lies of this reality. You can never change a lie. It will always be a lie. It is where people tell you, "This and this is my issue," and they carry it around all their lives as they have decided that it is their issue. They agree and align to that fact and resist and react to it at the same time and go further and further down into the problem. Nothing else, nothing different and nothing greater can come into their awareness.

I had a patient who came to me because she was convinced that anger is her problem and that she would have to work hard to get rid of it. She had many people tell her what an angry person she was and that she indeed had a big problem that needed psychological counseling. Here she was, looking at me with resentment and convincing me with all her might how angry a person she is. She used her body and her voice in a way that should have induced fear in me.

With the awareness that her anger is not the problem, I met her for our first session with all my barriers down, not agreeing or aligning with the fact that her anger is her problem, nor resisting and reacting to her angry way of approaching me. She was surprised. She had never met anyone who met her with no point of view and who was in total allowance of her, even though she had decided what a terrible person she was. Her astonishment about being received the way she was made her question what was going on and opened a door where I could show her a different possibility.

We started the journey by first getting her into allowance of her anger by releasing the judgments and resistance against her anger. That changed her point of view and allowed her to let go of making herself wrong. The space opened up where she got access to herself in a totally different way. Beneath all the anger she had made real all her life was this enormous potency: A strong, creative woman who has been made wrong all her life for being different and independent. Once she spotted the lie called anger she could receive what she is truly capable of and know the gift she is. What showed up after that was truly astonishing. This woman turned out to be totally different than she ever could imagine she was. She changed her whole life, career, way of living and being.

Everywhere we resist, react, agree, align, have any point of view or judgment of what is right or wrong we limit our awareness of what is actually going on, and we limit our capacities of changing what we would like to change. Perceiving everything as just an interesting point of view gives you the freedom of you. In fact, everything can be right or wrong depending on who is judging: culture, age, past experience, etc. Looking at everything as just an interesting point of view allows for relaxation to show up where things that were judged as valuable and real can lose their significance and importance.

This is the space of allowance where everything is just an interesting point of view, all is included and nothing is judged. From that space, my client accessed the possibility of receiving herself and started the journey of becoming aware of who she really is and capable of. The process of changing her reality and creating a different life started. With every session she increased her willingness to release the lies of anger and limitations, opened up to possibility, and to being grateful for who she is. Gratitude is a relaxed state of being. It is being in allowance of what is and what was and the joyful awareness of what is possible.

So instead of having the target of handling anger, hate, fury, guilt and shame in your life or in therapy, a more effective approach is being in allowance of what is and discovering what these implants are distracting us from. How can this be done? The ultimate invitation for others to be more of themselves is for us to be more of ourselves. Be you and change the world.

The distractor implants are designed to control, impel a point of view, and limit the possibility to choose. Anger and guilt are perfect ways to control others and to be controlled by others. When somebody blames someone for something without asking a question, usually both people function from autopilot: They feel bad and there is no way out.

When something like that shows up in your life, know that what you have in front of you is a lie, a distraction from what is truly possible, from the potency and power and the being you truly be. Letting go of all the distractor implants allows you to have ease and infinite choice. Without anger, guilt and shame, how are others able to control you?

If we all would be who we truly are, wouldn't this reality have to change from what it is now?

Ask yourself:

What power and potency am I not willing to be and receive that I am hiding behind anger?

What am I not willing to be that I am hiding underneath the guilt and shame?

Does asking these questions make you feel lighter? Somewhere in your universe does it open up a knowing that there is a greater possibility?

I worked with a very beautiful young woman who suffered from getting red in the face any time somebody started talking to her. She told me that men lusted after her and she was so embarrassed that her face would flush when they spoke. She tried to avoid eye contact, but every time others looked at her she went away ashamed. This led to sadness and a feeling like she had failed. She was very troubled by this.

So I asked her, what are you not willing to be and receive? She looked at me with surprise and said, "Lust. And the fact that the men looking at me want to sleep with me."

"So you are not willing to receive the energy that they deliver at you?" I asked.

"No," she said.

"So, you are putting up a barrier to receiving that energy?"

"Yes," she said.

"So what's up with that? What are you not willing to be?"

"Well, I don't want to be a slut," she replied.

"Not being willing to be a slut makes you put up the barriers to not receiving that energy. Everything you are not willing to be you defend against and cut off your being and receiving of that energy and people with that energy. Have you decided that being a slut is a wrongness?"

She said, "Oh yes."

"So let me ask you a question: 'Truth, would allowing yourself to be a slut be fun for you?'" She started to laugh uncontrollably and her body relaxed. That was a very clear "Yes." "Not being willing to be what you have decided is wrong, is what limits you from what you can be and receive. It's not about going out and sleeping with everybody, it's about allowing yourself to receive, to be the sexualness you truly are and have fun and enjoy yourself and others lusting after you. And how much more money could you create by allowing yourself to receive everything and everybody lusting after you?"

I asked her to get the energy of being a slut and to receive the lust that men deliver at her, and put down all her barriers and receive all that, in all its intensity and in every cell of her body. She was surprised and happy about what showed up: The awareness of how much energy she used to make sure she would not receive what she had decided is wrong. And the intensity of what was possible for her to be and receive and the happiness and joy that opened up in her world was incredible. She blossomed and enjoyed people looking at her, had a totally different connection to her body, and did not have a point of view any more whether she would turn red or not.

These distractor implants are what distract you from what is actually going on. Once you spot them, you can identify them as distractor implants and ask yourself if you would like to continue to buy the lie that you have a problem, or ask a question to change what is going on. Distractor implants are the answers that lead you to a dead end. An answer disempowers, a question empowers and opens up doors for a different possibility.

Next time something feels heavy, ask if a distractor is running the show of your life at that moment. Just say in your head, "All the distractor implants running the show right now and everything underneath, I destroy and uncreate." Then use the clearing statement. *Right and wrong, good and bad, pod and poc, all nine, shorts, boys and beyonds.*

You agreed and aligned and resisted and reacted to them in the first place. If you can do that, you also have the potency to undo them. Ask yourself:

What is actually possible beyond the distractor implants?

What are you distracting yourself from being and receiving with the distractor implants?

How much of your potency, the infinite being you are, the joy and the ease are you hiding underneath these implants to convince yourself that you are as normal and real as you have decided you are supposed to be?

What is possible for you to be and receive that you have not acknowledged?

CHAPTER TEN

DEFENDING—YOU IN YOUR CASTLE

Defending points of view and the rightness and the wrongness of what people think and feel is a big part of this reality. In most conversations you hear yourself and others defending your position and your point of view. You fight for your right for whatever you have decided is true and real. There is no freedom in defending. It keeps you in a constant state of judgment and fight. It keeps you busy and it keeps you paranoid, waiting for the attack.

What positions are you defending?

The position of being a woman, a man, a mother, a daughter, a good person, a bad person, a poor person, a rich person.

What have you decided you are, that you keep defending as though that would eventually give you you?

Everything that is, will you destroy and uncreate it? Thank you.

Right and wrong, good and bad, pod and poc, all nine, shorts, boys and beyonds.

Over the years I have met so many people who have told me about their problems, saying they would like to get over them, yet they keep defending them over and over, coming up with all kinds of reasons and justifications for why they have problems and why it is hard or not possible to get over them. Whenever something like that comes up, you are defending your problems.

What else are you defending?

That life is hard? That creating money with ease is not possible? That your body hurts as you get older? These are all defensive positions.

In psychology we learn that defense is healthy and required. There are theories about all kinds of defense systems and how they can be harmful, but they are also signs of adaption. Question is, would you like to adapt to this reality or would you like to be you, even if it does not match what is considered as normal in this reality? Adaption, or the freedom of being you?

The freedom of being you does not mean that you are going to be put in a loony bin. Otherwise I would be there already. Instead I work there and I change reality by being me beyond the adaption of this reality. How? When you are being you beyond defending who you are, then you are inviting change instead of fight. When I work with clients, everybody is invited to the possibilities beyond this reality without being forced to change. That is being the catalyst for a different future.

Whatever you are defending becomes the limitation you cannot overcome. If you have decided that you have to go to work every day and that you do not have enough money, you will defend that point of view every single day, convincing yourself that you are right in your point of view. "See again, more bills; see again, no lottery winning; see I did not get that bonus either this year...." or whatever it is for you.

Scan through your life. Where are you defending your limitations that leaves you in the no-choice universe?

Everything that is, will you destroy and uncreate it? Thank you.

Right and wrong, good and bad, pod and poc, all nine, shorts, boys and beyonds.

Whatever you defend eliminates choice and possibility. Whatever you are defending you cannot change. If you are defending your problems with your body or money or depression or whatever you define as your problem, you have already created it so solid as an invention that you are defending that very problem, and with that, keeping it in place without ever being able to change it. Coming out of defense allows for a different possibility. So keep on running that process.

You do not have to go through your whole life and analyze everywhere you are defending, you can just ask this question:

What defended position am I choosing that I truly could be refusing that if I would refuse it, would give me the freedom to be me?

This will bring up all the places and areas where you are defensive, everything that you are aware of and everything you are not aware of, everything you can put words to, and also all the limitations you cannot put words to. Simply ask that question and allow the energy to come up which will automatically be all the defensiveness you are choosing in your whole life. Then you just say:

I will now destroy and uncreate it all.

Right and wrong, good and bad, pod and poc, all nine, shorts, boys and beyonds.

Do that many times, for a couple of weeks, so you can clear as many layers as possible. During that time you will, more than ever, become aware of all the places you are choosing to defend any position. In all kinds of situations you will notice when and where you choose to defend. Once you are aware of it you can change it. So do not judge you, just because you notice all the places you are choosing defense.

How much are you defending that you have a problem so you are considered normal, because being without any problem is considered not normal and not possible? Are you aware that in this world people just assume that it is normal to have a problem and if you do not have one, you create one to be part of the "normal" team. I see this all the time with my clients. They get better and better, they enjoy living, everything starts to show up the way they always asked for, and then when they are about to explode into something even greater, they create a problem of some sort to defend the position that one is supposed to have a problem so they are still connected to this normal reality. Do you have to be connected to this reality? Or can you be aware of it, include it and create your reality?

Are you trying to be normal by being grumpy and having problems? Being normal is when you are not being happy and cheerful all the time. If you would be happy and cheerful all the time, people would ask you if you are insane. Being normal is fitting in the standard deviation, two standard deviations on the plus side and two standard deviations on the minus side. That is a statistical model for normality called the bell curve.

The zero point is where the majority of people are. Two points—two standard deviations on the right side—indicate when you are above average. Two standard deviations on the left side indicate when you are below average. If you fit somewhere on that scale—whether you are above average happy or below average happy—you are still normal. Many people like to play that game. If they had a period in their lives when they were above average happy, they notice that they are on their way off the scale, which is not normal anymore for them. So they create a problem, which means jumping to the below average scale. This is where they create a problem to even out the success they just had. Same with money and business or anything else. One cannot be too successful, just wait for the fall, is what we have learned.

What if you could be off the scale? What if you could be the total deviant in all areas of your life?

Are you defending against having it too easy in life? If you are smiling now, it is obviously true for you. Your body is letting you know. Bodies are so aware. You would probably not be reading this book if you would not be interested and asking for more ease.

People create problems by defending the past and are in that way creating their future. Every time you say something like, "Last time I was in this situation it did not turn out well," or "In my previous relationship I was cheated on, so I have trouble trusting people," you defend the past to create your future. Nothing different or greater can be created than the past you try to overcome.

How much are you trying to prove how nice you are
and that you would not do harm to anybody? How much
of your time and energy are you using to smile and to cen-
sure what you are saying and doing to prove that you are a
good human being? That is defending against being mean
and vicious. Are you really mean and vicious, or have you
somehow at some point decided that if people found out
how weird you really are, they would run away screaming
and you would be all alone? Isn't it time to let that insane
point of view go? Will you destroy and uncreate all that?
Thank you.

Right and wrong, good and bad, pod and poc, all nine, shorts,
boys and beyonds.

I have met many people who defend their insanity,
because they have chosen it. You can ask them about their
childhood and you will find all kinds of things that sound
like probable causes as to why they are the way they are.
Is this really relevant? All reasons and so-called causes are
the reasons and justifications that defend the point of view
that people do not have the potency to choose something
different. People who choose insanities and problems do so
because it works for them in some way. It creates a place
where they know who they are; it has a value that works for
them. There is nothing wrong with that. It is just a choice.

I had a patient who told me after a couple of sessions
how much happier she is now and that she is aware of all
kinds of possibilities for her future and that she is inspired
to work and do what she always wanted to do. Her life
started to expand very quickly. Just when she was about
to institute her new reality she chose to become depressed
and she started to be angry with me. We talked about it and
she could see that she invented the depression and anger to

prove to me and herself that she could not do it. It became clear to her that she was defending her depression and mental illness. Being aware of that, she could no longer deny that she has choice.

In psychiatry I meet many patients who choose to be insane. They usually just come for one session and they never come back. Why? Because they know I am opening the door to where they know that they have choice, and where they will not be able to deny anymore that their insanity and problems is their creation and they would rather continue being insane. Again, this is just a choice.

What if you could come out of defending your points of view and your judgments? How much more freedom would you have? Would you rather be right or free?

Would you rather be right and credible in this reality or have the freedom of being you, even if you would lose fitting in? How much would you be able to create what you truly desire? What are you choosing?

CHAPTER ELEVEN

YOUR "DISORDERS" ARE ACTUALLY SUPERPOWERS

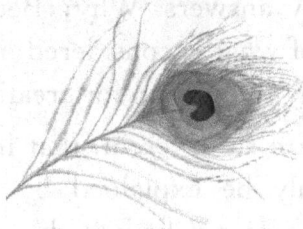

O ver the years of meeting many people with OCD (obsessive compulsive disorder) and ADHD (attention deficit hyperactive disorder) and autism, psychosis and bipolar, I soon realized that the old paradigm of considering these diagnoses as handicaps did not work. In fact it made me blind to look for the wrongness in the people I meet. It did not make sense to me. I would meet these people whose brilliance was so remarkable and the perspective I was handed in my education was to look for what was not working. I wondered how these people could be considered handicapped. Their creativity makes every intelligence test pale in comparison.

As a psychologist I do a lot of neuropsychological testing to get more information and to find out which diagnosis people have. These are standardized tests that describe what is normal, which means where the majority of the population functions, and they describe what is outside of the range of normality. The tests are a bunch of questions that people are supposed to answer, and if they answer them according to what is considered right they get a score, otherwise they don't.

Working with people with OCD, autism and ADHD, it has been a blast to see what wonderful, creative answers I receive to the test questions. Yet there are few scores for brilliant and funny answers. Why? Because they do not fit into the norm of what is considered right answers. But these people get my thumbs up for creativity and humor.

These people are so different, that in this reality their difference can only be explained by considering them handicapped. They do not fit into the standards of right-ness, which means they are deviant to what is normal. Their difference does not make sense to "normal" people. It is not logical enough. So the conclusion is: There must be some-thing wrong.

People with these diagnoses learn early on that there is something wrong with them and that they should learn how to fit in as well as possible. Today it is very common for them to get medications to take away what is called their symptoms and to make them fit into this reality. Every time I met someone who got medicated for their symptoms, they were more unhappy than before. They no longer had a sense of themselves. They said it was like being in a bubble they could not get out of.

Being acknowledged for their greatness and realizing that what is called their symptoms is actually a possibility, made most of my patients stop medicating and to learn to use their difference to their advantage.

For instance, a young man was diagnosed with ADHD and OCD for having all kinds of rituals which he had to go through in a certain order each day, all day long to maintain calm. It took him ages to get anywhere because he had to complete his rituals first. He was so troubled by that, and his family felt hopeless. They did not know what to do.

I met with him and he told me all the ways he thought he was wrong. He said he wouldn't be able to do anything with his life. He hardly got out of the house with all his rituals like washing his hands ten times and walking around the house in a certain order, and putting on his clothes in a certain order. If he did anything slightly different or if he got interrupted, he had to do it all over again until it was perfect.

On top of that he was hyperactive. He got medication and very soon realized that he did not need it. He told me that he felt so empowered and realized how amazing he is and that he has so much more potency than those little pills. He turned out to be one of the most funny and creative people I have met. He started a new education at college and now he works with children. Working in that environment with intensity and high tempo matches his energy, and he is happy.

How did he change from being troubled to creating his life?

By acknowledging who he truly is. By unbuying the lie that there is anything wrong with him. By inviting himself to know what he knows. By getting the information he needed and learning the tools to use his superpowers to his advantage.

Acknowledging who you truly are and what you are capable of works like magic. Getting over the wrongness of you and realizing that you are so much more than the mess you thought you were is what allows you to open the door to a totally different possibility. This is how I work with my clients: I perceive and know who they are and what they are capable of beyond the wrongness that they make real.

Imagine being in the presence of someone who does not judge you and who has no point of view about you or that you should change in any way. Someone who is aware of the you that you have not yet chosen to be. Notice how that relaxes you and your body? It's kind of like being in nature where the trees and the ocean are there to contribute to you and your body, with no point of view that you should be any different.

What if You could be that for You?

What energy, space and consciousness can you and your body be that allows you to be the nurturing, caring space that you and your body truly be?

Everything that does not allow that to show up—will you destroy and uncreate it, times a godzillion?

Right and wrong, good and bad, pod and poc, all nine, shorts, boys and beyonds.

Run that clearing a couple of times to remind you of the space that is possible for you to be and receive.

What is ADHD?

ADHD (attention deficit hyperactive disorder) is a set of implants that create what is called the ADHD symptoms; hyperactivity and attention deficit. Implants are everything you agree and align with and resist and react to that create all implanted points of view and limitations. These implants are easily removed if, and only if, the person chooses to remove them. You can use the clearing statement for that.

If the person would rather hold on to those limitations because they provide secondary gain because others take care of them, or people's expectations are lower, the implants cannot be removed. It is a choice the person has to make.

The possibility that is available beyond the implants is to fully receive the capacities that ADHD offers. People with this diagnosis have enormous potential in being aware and being able to have many projects going on at the same time, and managing them all with ease. I have had many patients with ADHD who had one or more businesses and created them with brilliance and enormous creativity. For the maintenance part of their business, for example, bookkeeping, they required staff. Being aware of the generative and creative energy that ADHD allows, invites you to be it and use it to your advantage. Be aware what is fun for you and who you can add to your life to take care of the things you do not have fun or ease with.

Many people with ADHD have "a worrier" in their family or among their friends. They are aware of the worry and think it is their own. One of my patients had a mother who worried about him excessively. He suffered from hypochondria, but when he became aware that his constant worry about being sick was actually his mother's worry, the hypochondria went away.

One suggestion people with ADHD get is that they should do one thing at a time and finish one project before they start a new one. That actually does not work. I know that as I have had many clients with ADHD. What works is to have as much going on as possible. That matches the generative, creative energy these people have. The more they have going on, the more relaxed they are. When you let go of the point of view that it can be too much for you, then you can receive what is possible for you. Your point of view creates your reality.

Having the TV or music on along with Facebook and email while doing homework or writing a report, and taking a break to eat or talk to a friend might work best for people with ADHD. And yet that is considered wrong in this reality. You should do one thing at a time and not have too much going on otherwise you will get stressed. Is that really true? Does that make you feel lighter? Ask what works for You? What do You know? What if what you know and what you are capable of is beyond this reality?

What is OCD?

OCD, or obsessive compulsive disorder, is an incredible awareness and the defense against the ease of the space of picking up other people's thoughts, feelings and emotions. Not buying thoughts, feelings, emotions as yours and not having a point of view about them, or trying to do anything with them, would allow you to have ease with it. Defending against your awareness creates a contraction. The point of view that many people have is that they have to protect themselves from all the information they pick up. People do a lot to know less.

OCD is about having rituals and routines that have to be done and if they are done wrong, they have to be done again until the routine and the ritual is done perfectly. It is occupying oneself with doing certain behaviors to avoid being aware. You do not have to have an OCD diagnosis to know what I am talking about. How many to-do lists do you create every day to avoid being and receiving what is truly possible for you?

What if OCD is actually not a handicap, but a capacity of intense awareness of this reality? This would mean an ability to be aware of what is going on in other people's universes, thoughts, feelings and emotions. Not being aware of the stimuli these people take in creates a feeling of overwhelm. In order to function in this reality, they create a strategy of getting by and of dealing with everything they are aware of.

In this reality, we are not taught to just receive information and be in allowance of it. We have to make sense of all the information around us. We have to make up an opinion, a point of view, understand it, judge what is right and wrong, and draw conclusions. People with OCD are very aware of this. Their way of functioning in this reality, their way of getting by with all the information they are receiving, is doing what everybody else is doing in this reality. They come up with a way of judging what is required to do for everything to work out fine. The rituals, the rigidity that is observed with people who have the diagnosis OCD would be an attempt to make sure all chaos is taken care of and that everything is secure. Their point of view is to ensure that they do the ritual right, make sure that all is well, and that nobody gets hurt.

People with OCD are also extremely aware. They pick up other people's thoughts, feelings and emotions from their surroundings even if these people are physically far away from them. They buy these thoughts, feelings and emotions as theirs, thinking that everything they are aware of applies to them. Imagine how much information that is and what making everything relevant to you creates. You would look for a way to make sense of it all and to find a way to handle all that information.

One tool you can use when you "feel" overwhelmed is to ask yourself this question:

Is this really relevant to me?

Just because you pick up information from all around you does not mean that everything is relevant to you. It is like watching TV and trying to make sense of every word every person says on each channel. It is just information, and most of it has nothing to do with you. Another tool that is very helpful is the question:

Who does this belong to?

For everything that is heavy, when you ask this question and it gets lighter, that is an indication it is not yours. When it does not lighten up, ask, "Did I create this as mine?" If you get a "yes," say:

Everything that is, everywhere I have created this as mine, I destroy and uncreate it, times a godzillion.

Right and wrong, good and bad, pod and poc, all nine, shorts, boys and beyonds.

One of my patients who had been depressed for many years had tried all kinds of medication and all kinds of therapy, and nothing could change her depression. She stopped talking and it was obvious that she was dying. I was working with her and one day she came in and looked at me with a smile. That woman had not smiled in years. She looked at me and said, "I am happy today, I came from home and realized that the things that were in my head and the things that made me heavy have nothing to do with me. It's not me; it has never been mine." From that day on, the woman started to create her life like never before. She had all kinds of plans of what she would like to explore and do. All from a little question.

Asking this question allows you, more and more, to be aware of the space you are and to be it no matter where you are, or who you are with. You no longer have to choose an exit strategy of settling down on a lonely island or meditating in a cave for 20 years to have peace. You can have it now in the middle of the craziest, loudest city. And you being that space changes the people around you. As you become that space and ease and peace being you, the people around can no longer hold on to their insanity as much as they could when you played insanity together with them. Oh the joy. Imagine what a different world we all can create.

What are you doing to not be aware? What are you occupying yourself with to avoid being, knowing, perceiving and receiving? What is truly possible for you and your life with your awareness that you have not yet acknowledged?

Being aware is receiving all information from everything and everyone. That is not always comfortable. You are aware of the happiness and the sadness and everything else people are functioning from. The possibility with being conscious and aware is that you can have it all with ease. You can receive all the information and use it to your advantage to create your life. How? By stopping to pretend that there is anything wrong with you. Acknowledge that there is nothing wrong with anything and that the information you are picking up is just an interesting point of view.

Would you rather walk around blindfolded in the world, avoiding what you know and hoping you get it right some day, or would you like to open your eyes and receive all information to know where you can go next that creates greater possibilities for you?

What is Autism?

There are many misunderstandings and lack of information about autism in the world. Autism is considered a handicap in this reality. The point of view is that there is something wrong with autistic people.

What if there is nothing wrong with them?

Working with autistic people turned everything I learned during my education upside down. I was astonished about the lack of information and incorrect information I was taught. What I found in my work with autistic people is the possibility and the contribution people with autism are to this world. They truly are different. Being different is not considered a valuable trait in this reality. Being autistic means being extremely different in the way of being and functioning. It means being extremely aware of everything and everyone around them all the time.

"Normal" people usually have their barriers and defenses up. The point of view is that it protects you from what is going on around you. It makes you safe and gives you a sense of self. People with autism do not have such defenses.

Asking questions and exploring what else is possible, I found that the necessity of defenses is an approach to life that does not work so well. It does not create change, nor does it make things better. Defending keeps you in a constant wait for attack and fight mode. When something does not work, I look at it and ask questions to get more information to know what else is possible that would work even better. That is being pragmatic. (Oh, wait a second, this book *is* titled *Pragmatic Psychology!*)

The approach of having defenses in place actually gives us less of ourselves. It creates the point of view that it is possible to be negatively affected by other people and it creates the necessity to constantly defend one's territory and personal space.

How much are you defending your personal space at all times, as though that is required for you to be safe and have peace? How well is that working for you? And how much of that makes you feel tired and alone and not connected to other people, the earth, nature and your body? Would you consider a different possibility?

All the necessities of barriers and defense and all the points of view that you have created holding that in place and everything you agree and align and resist and react to, will you now destroy and uncreate all of that? Thank you.

Right and wrong, good and bad, pod and poc, all nine, shorts, boys and beyonds.

Lowering your barriers allows you to receive everything and be connected to everything. When I changed my point of view and let go of my necessity of barriers and allowed myself to be vulnerable, my whole life changed. I got how much potency there is in having my barriers down. I had access to me more than ever before.

When I work with singers and actors and people who desire to have their voice be heard, we often practice lowering the barriers to allow a greater connection to their audience. As they allow others to see and experience their gifts, their gifts are then better received. Their voice changes instantaneously without having to learn any technique. They are present as themselves and everyone and everything gets to gift to them. This is a contribution that creates a different possibility for the world.

I worked with a woman who said that she was afraid of speaking in public. She went on stage at one of my workshops and the first thing I asked her was to lower her barriers. She did and she started to burst into laughter and total joy. I asked her what she became aware of and she said, "Oh my god, I always thought that I was afraid of being seen and heard and that I just wanted to hide from the world and now I just realized that all of that was a lie and that I love speaking. And what I thought was fear actually is excitement and the joy of being seen and heard."

The woman later told me that she went to a big fashion show speaking in front of a huge audience and enjoyed it and allowed it to change her world. All of this resulted from lowering her barriers and allowing herself to receive herself.

What could you find out about you, lowering all your barriers and receiving you?

Everything that does not allow you to be, know, perceive and receive that in totality, will you destroy and uncreate it all? Thank you.

Right and wrong, good and bad, pod and poc, all nine, shorts, boys and beyonds.

Being connected to everything and everyone allows you to receive all the information you require all the time. Having your barriers down contributes to the energy your body needs. Receiving everything creates the space where the body requires less sleep and less food. People think that energy comes primarily from food and sleep. Really? How many times have you slept and ate a great deal and you were still tired? How many times have you eaten and felt more tired afterwards? How often have you forced your body to sleep, having the point of view that this is what you need in order to have the energy you need to get by?

Everything that is and all the points of view you have about the necessity of sleep and food that override your awareness, will you now destroy and uncreate it all? Thank you.

Right and wrong, good and bad, pod and poc, all nine, shorts, boys and beyonds.

Letting go of all those points of view allows you to ask questions that give you the information about what you and your body truly require. "Body, would you like to eat now? Body, what would you like to eat? How much?" Your body will give you the awareness about what it requires and when. Your body talks to you all the time. Once you start asking questions, and start listening, you will have an easier time hearing what it tells you.

Having your barriers down allows you to be the magic you truly are. It allows you to be and receive infinitely. How much of your financial wealth are you diminishing with the barriers you are putting up to receiving? Are you aware of the barriers you have up and don't know what to let in? They are protecting you from everything, even money. They do not know that their job is to let all the money you desire to come into your life. *Everything that is, will you destroy and uncreate it? Thank you.*

Right and wrong, good and bad, pod and poc, all nine, shorts, boys and beyonds.

Are you starting to get a sense of what barriers you have created in your life? They are based on the lie that you need them. Question: Is that true? Does that point of view make you feel lighter? Does it create more in your life or less?

Being vulnerable is not a "wrongness." It is a "strongness". It is being and receiving everything without a point of view that anything or anyone can hurt you. It is like being a marshmallow. Everything just bounces back. Having barriers up means that there is always something to fight against which takes a lot of energy. There is nothing that can hurt you, unless you have the point of view that it can hurt you. Again—your point of view creates your reality.

Being vulnerable and receiving everything does not mean that you take things on or that you have to hold on to them, carry them around or store them in your body. It means that you are aware of them and let them go through you like the wind.

What does all of that have to do with autism?

Awareness about barriers gives you a different perspective on how autistic people function. It invites you to a different point of view where being aware of everything at all times is not a "wrongness" but a "strongness."

Being autistic is not having any filters and barriers to all the information and awareness. It is kind of like not having a skin. It is all there and all at the same time.

The common point of view is that autistic people have a lack of emotions and feelings and that this is a handicap.

How much more can you be and receive you when you are not thinking and feeling and emoting?

Thoughts, feelings and emotions are based on polarity —good and bad, right and wrong. You are always on one pole or the other and never have the freedom of being.

Are you willing to find out who you are beyond thoughts, feelings and emotions? It is such an adventure. It is the place where you have choice, true choice.

If it is a "yes" for you, run this clearing as often as possible:

What invention are you using to create the thoughts, feelings, emotions and upset you are choosing?

Everything that is, will you destroy and uncreate it all? Thank you.

Right and wrong, good and bad, pod and poc, all nine, shorts, boys and beyonds.

Autistic people perceive everything at all times, which means that they pick up the information, thoughts, feelings, emotions at all times and everything that is said and not said verbally.

I have a friend who worked with a mother and her autistic kid and they were sitting in the living room when the kid looked at the fridge and, without words, let the mother know that he wanted some orange juice. The mother got the information and as she was on her way to the fridge she asked, with words, if he wanted some orange juice and the kid started to scream. My friend asked the mother, "So is your son frustrated right now because he knows that you already know what he wants and that you asked him a question about something you already knew? "Yes" was the awareness. His mother's question made the kid frustrated as his mother made herself slower by pretending not to know what she knew.

That is an example about how autistic people function. They communicate with words and without words. Words are not a necessity in their world, and they know that you know, and they know when you are making yourself slower and more stupid than you are, which causes much of their frustration and tantrums.

Funny how what looks like tantrums and upsets with autistic people actually is not about anything being wrong but a way of telling you something, an information about a possibility. What if we let go of the perception something is wrong and receive the possibility that we hide behind it?

It is said that autism means a disability in communication. How incorrect is that point of view?

We all communicate with and without words. How many times have you known who was calling you before you picked up the phone or checked the display? When you are thinking of a person, how many times is that person actually thinking of you and requiring something from you, and you concluded that it is you who is thinking of that person?

We know so much more than we think. Thinking is just a minor form of knowing. Knowing is faster and quicker. Being with autistic people is amazing and a great way to practice your knowing and your communication beyond the necessity of words.

I play with that all the time in my practice. I have a psychology test that I use with my patients. We play with it. It is not intended to be played with—it is supposed to be very serious, but that does not work for me. I love to use it to empower people to know that they know. This test is like a puzzle; there is a picture where one piece is missing and there are five answers to choose and one of them is the piece that is missing in the picture.

First, I ask the client which one is the right piece, which means that I ask them to use their brain and think and figure out the right answer. Then I ask how that worked for them and usually the answer is that it was hard work, or that their head or their eyes hurt from concentrating on the picture and figuring out the right answer. Then we do it again with another puzzle. This time I ask the client to not think and to use their knowing and ask the puzzle which one piece is the correct one that is missing.

What results is that most of the time the answer the client comes up with is correct and the client is surprised how fast and easy it was. They say their brain was telling them that it cannot be that easy and fast, and that they are supposed to think some more to come up with the right answer. What they learn is that they can trust their awareness. Then we do one more round, and again I ask the client to use their knowing, and I tell them I will have the correct answer in my head and they just need to take it from there. That is a fun way of exploring what it is like to pick up someone else's thoughts. And it works.

So what capacities of knowing and picking up other people's thoughts, feelings and emotions do you have that you have not yet acknowledged?

Everything that does not allow you to be, know, perceive and receive that, will you destroy and uncreate it please? Thank you.

Right and wrong, good and bad, pod and poc, all nine, shorts, boys and beyonds.

Allowing you to know helps a lot when you communicate with autistic people. It creates so much ease and peace in their universe as you do not pretend to be more stupid than you truly are.

What if you could take everything you are aware of and use it as a contribution to your life and your body? How much more ease would that create in your life?

A mother who I worked with has an autistic son and she complained about the fact that he did not get ready in time in the mornings. She used every strategy she could come up with to manipulate him into getting ready, but he refused.

She asked me for help, so I told her to telepathically give her son pictures, like a fast slideshow, of what she would like him to do, and what the day is going to look like. She had never done such a thing and did not know about communicating telepathically, so she thought she would at least try it.

Having nothing to lose and not really knowing how she should do it, in her head she just got pictures of how the day should look and gave her son the download of that. The woman was surprised beyond belief how well that worked. Her son relaxed and got ready just in time before they had to leave. They continued communicating that way and their relationship improved dynamically.

Autistic people have amazing capacities beyond what this reality can grasp or understand. They function beyond the norm and way off the scale of what we call normal, and they are so different that the only way of making sense of them in this reality is to call autism a handicap.

That applies also for ADHD, OCD and other so-called diagnoses. All these diagnoses are a mutation of the species into a different way of functioning that does not make sense, and people want to understand, figure out and explain what they cannot understand, and everything that is different has to be wrong. Interesting point of view. Why does difference have to be wrong?

What difference are you and have you made wrong that if you be it, would change your whole life?

Everything that is will you destroy and uncreate it? Thank you.

Right and wrong, good and bad, pod and poc, all nine, shorts, boys and beyonds.

I am writing a lot about autism as it is one of the least understood phenomena in psychology besides schizophrenia and psychosis. So what if instead of labeling it as a "wrongness," we took another look and asked, "What is actually possible here? What can we learn here that we have not acknowledged?"

Autistic people do not function from thoughts, feelings or emotions. Those do not make sense to them. Thinking, feeling and emoting are the lower harmonics of being, knowing, perceiving and receiving. Thinking, feeling and emoting is the contracted version of being, receiving, knowing and perceiving as they are based on polarity. There is always a positive and a negative side. That is not the case with being, knowing, receiving and perceiving. They are not based on polarity. It is the expansive way we can operate.

In this reality we have learned there is great value in thinking, feeling and emoting. Interesting, isn't it exactly that which causes problems and keeps us locked in constant suffering? It is quite easy to go beyond thinking, feeling, and emoting and function from being, receiving, perceiving, and knowing. It is faster and makes life a lot easier as you are not the effect of polarity anymore, of the good and the bad. Good or bad ceases to be relevant and everything is just an interesting point of view and you have choice.

For autistic people it is very painful to be forced to function from the lower harmonic of thinking, feeling and emoting. It is like forcing a big round ball into a small square box. Their way of functioning from being, knowing perceiving and receiving makes them extremely aware of other people's points of view. They are very aware of all the information around them at all times.

Do not ask autistic people how they feel. If you ask them that, they will tap into all the people's feelings around them to figure out how they are supposed to feel. Ask them what they are aware of. When you notice that they are contracting and getting upset, ask them, "Who does this belong to? Is this yours?"

Asking those questions creates great relaxation for them as they are empowered to know that they are aware and that what they are aware of has nothing to do with themselves.

This is not only the case for autistic people. How many of the points of view and problems that you put on your shoulders every day are actually not yours?

Would you be willing to let go of everything that is not yours and return it to sender, without having to know who the sender is? Thank you.

I was working with a young man with Asperger's—a type of autism—and as soon as he applied the tool of asking "Who does this belong to?" and "Is this mine?" for every thought, feeling and emotion he thought was his, his whole world changed. He told me how much freedom that created for him and that he realized how different he is, and that there is nothing wrong with him, and that the way he is, is actually a great way of being.

He told me that he became aware that "normal" people create a lot of problems with their thinking and feeling and putting so much meaning to everything. He may not always know what is socially appropriate, but now that he no longer makes himself wrong when he notices people getting upset, he simply asks, "How are you? What is going on?

Can I help you in any way?" Most of the time that takes the wind out of angry people's sails.

He said he often feels like an alien, not getting what the fuss is about for most people and why people react in certain ways, but he does not bother anymore. He feels good about himself and knows that he is a contribution to the world just being who he is.

That is what makes my work so much fun.

Autism is a level of awareness you cannot turn off, but you try to find a way to live with the insanity of the people around you who do turn off their awareness. Autistic people have no off button. Turning off awareness does not make sense in their world.

Those who are functional autistics—which means they are autistic and have learned to seem normal and live a "normal" life—try to figure out where they need to put their awareness in order for it to work for others. They adjust themselves. That takes a lot of energy and requires a lot of effort to hide what they know, even from themselves, to fit into other people's realities.

Acknowledging that this is what they do, every time they interact with other people creates great freedom and invites choice. The possibility is to be all you are with everyone and say what other people can receive. You do not need to say what you know to people who cannot receive it. All they will do is resist you. As my friend, Gary Douglas, says, "Just for you, just for fun, never tell anyone."

Never diminish your awareness in favor of other people's points of view. You know what you know, no matter what other people say. What if you could receive what other people think and feel as an interesting point of view and not make it real or significant and know what you know?

I was at an airport the other day, getting ready to board. The staff were pretty nervous and wanted me to move faster. For a second I was on my way to hurry and move faster and I made the staff's point of view real. Then I asked myself what I know, received the awareness that we had time, acknowledged my knowing and relaxed. What showed up was that the staff started to relax too, and all was well. There was plenty of time before the plane was going to take off.

Acknowledging what you know creates more freedom and ease in your life and in other people's lives. It is the space where you no longer throw away your awareness in favor of other people's points of view.

Schizophrenia and Psychosis

Schizophrenia and psychosis are considered to be the more severe mental illnesses. They are supposed to primarily be cured with medication. There is no traditional therapy that can cure schizophrenia and psychosis.

People who have these diagnoses hear voices or see things that others do not see. They are usually very troubled by this. The common point of view is that these people must be sick and there must be something wrong with them. That is an answer that leaves no room for further exploration. No wonder there are no therapies that can facilitate a different possibility.

To create a different functional reality for people with these diagnoses, we have to begin with questions. What is it? What is possible with it? What is required to facilitate a different possibility for these people?

I have seen patients with schizophrenia and psychosis. One of them was a young woman who has always heard voices and seen people that other people do not see. She could see and hear people who were dead and did not have bodies anymore. She could talk to her deceased grandmother. When she was in her kitchen cooking food, she could sense people tapping on her shoulder who desired to talk to her.

The problem was she thought she was wrong and sick and that she had to cut off her knowing about what she was capable of. When she told me about the voices and what she saw, which took a lot of courage, I asked if she had a talent and ability of being aware of beings without bodies that she had not acknowledged. She smiled, started to laugh, and she and her body relaxed. Her whole universe lightened up and she opened the door to accessing herself and what she was capable of more than ever before. She let go of the point of view that there was anything wrong, and she was able to explore and enjoy her talents. She no longer required psychiatry.

Most people who work with patients diagnosed with psychosis and schizophrenia are somewhere aware that this is what is going on, but they never allow or dare to acknowledge it, as it totally goes beyond what is normal.

Is now the time for us to be courageous and see what is actually going on instead of chasing the tale of what is "normal" or scientifically proven? If we cannot help people and change what is going on into something greater, how good are the models and theories we have been taught? If it does not work, ask a question. If it does not work, ask and explore a different possibility. Be pragmatic. Be awake. Be courageous enough to look beyond the norm.

Following what others say, what science says, what other theories say, is maintaining the status quo and maintaining what people think is going on. Acknowledging what is truly going on has the potential of creating possibilities that empower people to know that they know. It has the potential of creating a different world and a sustainable future.

Entities

Working in psychiatry, this is something that shows up on a daily basis, whether you work with people who have been diagnosed with schizophrenia and psychosis or not. Entities, which means beings without bodies, talk to us all the time. Many people end up in psychiatry because they are aware of entities and have a lack of education on how to deal with them. As soon as they learn how to handle what they are aware of, diagnosis and mental illness are no longer relevant. They can have a sense of peace and ease with what they are aware of.

With many unexplainable situations where people have sudden breakdowns, you can ask if that has something to do with entities. People who take drugs, drink a lot or choose unawareness give their body up for rent, and entities can come in and take over.

I recently had a lady I worked with whose brother called me and said that his sister suddenly is totally different; she calls people and says weird stuff to them and just sits at home, and he does not know what to do. He asked me to check on her.

When I visited her in her home, she opened the door and her overall expression was confused and she was literally not being herself. So I sat down and asked her about what was going on. I asked if she would like to let go of whatever is not allowing her to be herself right now. She said yes and it really was a yes. People often say yes to letting go and what they mean is no.

While she was talking, I energetically connected to the entities in her body and removed them. She looked at me, smiled and thanked me. It turned out she had these entities in her body all the time, but something triggered them and she chose this time to let them go. She came to the office the next day, totally changed, being herself again.

Had I done normal psychology, she would have been transferred to a hospital for in-patient treatment and she would have received medication. What would that have created for her?

What I did was weird and wacky but it worked. That is being pragmatic, doing what works.

Some people are so-called portals, which means they are a big open door for entities. That is the case with schizophrenics. They have at some point chosen to be portals. Entities run through them like cars on a highway. You can see that when you talk to a person and suddenly it seems as if you're talking to somebody else, and then a few moments later, there is somebody else you notice. If the person chooses to let go of being a portal, it is very easy and fast to close a portal. Buildings can be portals too. They are places where you suddenly become very dizzy or notice something weird. Just reading this, you are aware of the energy I am talking about.

Ask yourself how many of the thoughts in your head are your own. When you have a hard time deciding what to do and there is one voice telling you to go in this direction and another voice wanting you to go in another direction, or the voices speak to you in "you" form, ask yourself, "Are these entities I am aware of?" How do you know if it is entities?

Ask, "Truth, am I aware of entities?" Does "yes" or "no" make you feel lighter? The one that makes you feel lighter is true for you.

Entities like to live in people's bodies. It is very common for one or more entities to be inside of a person's body. That is not a terrible thing. Entities are not more powerful than you. You are the one with the body, you are in charge!

How do you remove entities?

By connecting to the entities you would like to let go of and using this clearing sentence:

Truth who are you, truth who were you before that, truth who were you before that, truth who were you before that? (You say this until the energy changes.)

Truth who will you be in the future? Thank you, you can go now.

And all the magnetic imprints in the body, destroy and uncreate them.

Right and wrong, good and bad, pod and poc, all nine, shorts, boys and beyonds.

By asking "Who were you before that? Who will you be in the future?" you get the entity unstuck from their position in time. The magnetic imprints are the imprint the entity made in your body by being there.

Bipolar

Bipolar had a different name in the past and was called manic depression. It is where people have depressive (low) episodes and manic (high) episodes.

When I work with people who have been diagnosed with bipolar, I always ask myself, "Truth, is this really bipolar?" Many times my knowing says that it is not bipolar even if the person has been diagnosed. It is simply people who have been misunderstood and who have been happier than the norm. Being too happy makes people wonder what is wrong with you.

How much are you holding back your joy and happiness to not seem insane or too much?

Everything that is will you please destroy and uncreate it? Thank you.

Right and wrong, good and bad, pod and poc, all nine, shorts, boys and beyonds.

I know this is all so easy: Asking a question to find out what is truly going on instead of buying the conclusion that someone else created by giving the patient a diagnosis.

The low periods, or depression, are many times peoples' awareness of other people's and this reality's density. So many of the clients I meet are simply aware of what is going on in the world and buying it as theirs, creating it as theirs, and with that making themselves the effect of it. Using the "Who does this belong to?" tool creates a huge shift, as it acknowledges that the sadness they think is theirs really has nothing to do with them.

In one session you can change someone's life. Just by asking questions and acknowledging what is.

What I found with clients who have been diagnosed with bipolar, and I ask and I get a "yes" it is bipolar, is that the client is creating a conflictual universe, which means that they are constantly living in an either/or world. One of my clients had a conflictual universe with her sexuality, where she wanted to have a lot of sex and at the same time was disgusted by sex and wanted to be a nun.

Bipolar is constantly creating separation by wanting to be here, and not wanting to be here, wanting to have a body, and not wanting to have a body. In the high periods where everything is so fantastic, people feel like they are finally themselves. And yes, they somehow are the joy they truly are, and at the same time they create that joy as a state, a place they have to go to achieve that joy, rather than being a peaceful, beyond-the-doubt acknowledgment of who they already are. Facilitating the client to be, know, perceive, and receive that can create a huge change.

Joy is not a state to go to or achieve. It is what we already be. When you start to acknowledge that, there is no need to work hard to become joyful or try to feel good or prove to yourself that you are happy. You let go of the manic part of happiness and you get to be happy with great peace. True happiness is the awareness that there are always expanding possibilities.

In the psychiatric field there is a lot of unclarity with ADHD and bipolar. There are certain similarities. Both groups of people are very aware and have beyond the norm ups and downs. What I found is that setting a diagnosis is not really relevant as this is usually a way to find an answer. Instead, it helps to have the awareness with each individual person about what is going on, and in which way the person is creating their limitation. Is it mainly about conflictual universes or do they not know how to handle their awareness, or both, or something else?

Questions will lead you to know what is going on and to the choices that are available that create a different future.

CHAPTER TWELVE

OUT OF ABUSE

M any people have experienced abuse in one form or another. Sexual and verbal abuse are the ones that most people consider. There are so many other ways of abuse that we inflict on ourselves every day, like excessive thinking: Using your brain more than required to make sure you get it right and not wrong; eating more than your body requires, and not asking if, what and when your body would like to eat, living by the answers of this reality rather than by asking questions.

What is your personal favorite torture tool to use on yourself and your body on a daily basis? Would you consider letting that go and discovering a different way of entertaining yourself? How much are you using all those ways of abuse to stay busy, to fit in, to be like everybody else, to not be as potent as you truly are, to distract yourself from creating your authentic life?

Everything that is, will you now destroy and uncreate it all, please? Thank you.

Right and wrong, good and bad, pod and poc, all nine, shorts, boys and beyonds.

Abuse is kind of the operative state in this reality. What do I mean? Let's do a little experiment. We are talking about psychology. What would psychology be without experiments?

My kind of psychology is more like play experiment. Are you in?

Tap into the energy of abuse, which means allow yourself to have a download of what the energy of abuse is. You do not need to visualize or do anything for that, just perceive what the energy of abuse is. Get how that energy feels in your body. Where are you contracting right now? Where do you feel tense? How much space do you have right now?

Now feel into how much of that energy is the energy of this reality where everything is about conformity, being normal, being right, being like everybody else, doing the right thing, living the right life with the right job and the right man or woman and the right amount of money, avoiding being wrong, avoiding losing? How much contraction are you aware of right now in your body?

Welcome to this reality, ladies and gentlemen. And if you act now, you can have a life sentence in prison reality all for the price of you. A little joke on my part...or not.

How much do you have to abuse and torture yourself to be able to be part of this reality and make you feel you fit in here?

Everything that is, would you destroy and uncreate it all, please? Thank you.

*Right and wrong, good and bad, pod and poc, all nine, shorts,
boys and beyonds.*

Now let go of the energy of abuse and everybody you
just connected to, to know what abuse is. Thank you.

Are you more relaxed since you let go of that energy?
This exercise allows you to see that you are so aware of
energies all the time and that you can receive them at any
time, and let them go again, without effort or force, just by
choice. The more you play with that, the easier it will be.

Next time you are in the presence of that energy of
abuse, whether it is in the form of a person or a situation,
say to yourself, "Ah, here is this energy again, what would I
like to choose now?" You will not automatically make yourself the effect of it anymore since you are aware of what it
is. The awareness of what is going on is what creates a different possibility for you.

I was once in a relationship with a man who told me
how much he loved and adored me, and that I was the best
thing that happened to him, except every time he said that
I felt sick and heavy and very angry. For a while, I made
myself wrong for not being happy when he declared his
love for me. How can I get so angry when he tells me how
much he loves me; how wrong, terrible and cold am I?

After a while of this torture, I finally became smart
enough to use my own tools. So I asked, "What is going
on? What am I aware of here that I have not acknowledged? What lies are going on here spoken or unspoken?"
Asking what the lie is a great question when you get angry.

It did not take long until I got the information from
another friend that my partner who said he loved me so
much actually had huge resentments of me and what I

was doing in the world. When I got that information, I felt so light again and the anger disappeared. What I became aware of is that every time he would tell me how much he loved me and I got angry, I sensed that he was lying and that he did not love me at all but judged me for my very being. That awareness created so much space for me, and I asked myself, "Is this the kind of person I would like to hang out with? Who and what else can I choose that expands my world?"

Awareness of what is going on without making it wrong creates possibilities and choice.

Abuse—Are you a healer?

I had a client who had trouble creating relationships that worked for her and had difficulties enjoying her body and sex. During our sessions, for the first time she got to know this man who was kind to her, who treated her with regard, and she and her body could relax. She told me that she was ready to look at what was going on with her body, and her difficulties enjoying sex.

I asked her some questions about when the difficulties started and she said right around when she was raped when she was a young teenager. After that she did not like sex and had a disgust towards her body. I asked her how much of the rapist's anger had she locked into her body and had been holding onto since then. It was like her whole universe exploded when I asked her that question. She said, "Oh my god, that is what I have been doing."

We talked about how much hatred this man had for women, and I asked her if she wanted to heal that in him. She said, "That is one of the weirdest questions ever, but it totally makes me feel lighter." She became aware that with the choice she made, she ended the circle of abuse that this man had been doing.

A question you can ask is:

What awareness and what strength did I have at the time of the abuse that I have not acknowledged?

The point of view that she was the victim had locked her up and did not allow her body to enjoy being touched and limited her capacity to receive, which also was reflected in her monetary situation. She became aware of her healing capacities which she had been using against herself. She became aware of all the people around her that had anger and rage and hatred as their primary way of functioning. She knew she had the ability to take that out of those people's universes and bodies, and she locked that into her body by not acknowledging what she was doing.

When we asked questions around what was really going on, she could expand her awareness and know what healing capacities she has that she now can use to her advantage. She told me after our sessions that this changed her whole life and her body. Her boyfriend told her that he does not know what happened, but that even his whole way of being with his body and sex changed too.

I shared this example as it has many aspects that you can use. How much are you a healer and have been taking out the pain and suffering from other people's universes and bodies your whole life? Does this make you lighter right now? Does your body relax? Did you just take a deep breath or sigh? Or did that change anything else for you?

These are clues that there is something about this that is true for you. When you live your life, constantly taking out the pain and suffering out of people's bodies and universes without being aware of it, you take you out of choice and make yourself the effect of the things going on around you. Once you realize what you are capable of, you can use it to your advantage and start using that capacity to create your life rather than abusing yourself.

I used to feel drunk every time I was out at bars. My head would spin and I felt totally drunk without having had a sip of anything alcoholic. I finally asked my body what was going on, what my body was aware of and what capacities my body has that I have not acknowledged. (Great questions by the way, which I recommend you ask your body.) What I learned was that my body has the capacity to take out the alcohol from other people's bodies. Once I was aware of that, I could ask my body to not do that all the time, or if it does it, for it to be easy and light for me. Since then I never had trouble being around drunk people. If I choose, I can dissipate the alcohol in other people's bodies or I cannot do it. Now it is a choice.

What are you and your body capable of that you have not acknowledged that if you would acknowledge it, would give you the totality of you?

Everything that does not allow you to be, know, perceive and receive that, will you destroy and uncreate it all? Thank you.

Right and wrong, good and bad, pod and poc, all nine, shorts, boys and beyonds.

When you are aware of your talents and capacities you can start using them to your advantage instead of being the victim of everything you have not been willing to know about yourself.

Every time you make someone or something more powerful or valuable than you, you abuse yourself. How often do you come to the conclusion that someone else knows better than you, so you create justifications based on that person's education or position in society? "Oh, he is a doctor, he must know more than me."

What creation of you are you using to subordinate, absolve and resolve your awareness and choice in favor of other people's realities are you choosing?

Everything that is will you destroy and uncreate it? Thank you.

Right and wrong, good and bad, pod and poc, all nine, shorts, boys and beyonds.

Every time you say someone else knows better, you turn off your awareness and limit you and your life.

Knowing that you know and being aware of what you and your body are capable of, gets you out of abuse and opens the doors to infinite choice.

Welcome to the adventure called You.

CHAPTER THIRTEEN

DEPRESSION—THE GREATNESS OF YOU

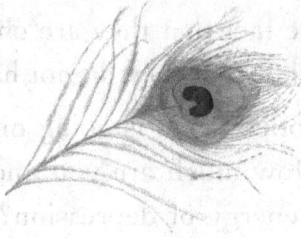

"As long as you are breathing, you can start all over again," is a song I am listening to while I am writing this. So true.

Depression is one of the major reasons why people seek psychiatry or psychological counseling. Most people have at some point in their life been depressed. It is the state where one has the point of view that nothing is joyful anymore and that there is no way anything can change. People say they have no energy to take even one step to create something different.

My clients often say they are victim to their depression, they have tried everything and nothing has helped, and they are too tired to be able to change their state. Sometimes I meet clients who are so depressed they have stopped talking.

Being depressed is one way of slowly dying. It is the state where one has given up and surrenders to the limitations of this reality. A slow suicide. How can I say this? Well, ask yourself, is depression something that takes you over or are people choosing to be depressed? Yes, they are choosing to be depressed. It is a passive way of existing and it is an active choice, yet not a conscious choice. Depressed people choose to surrender to life's limitations. They might not be aware of the fact that they are choosing this. Their point of view is rather that they do not have a choice.

Reading this notice, what is going on in your universe and your body? How much are you and your body right now aware of the energy of depression? Is this a familiar energy to you? Now instead of fighting it and trying to stop it, lower all your barriers, even more and more, and be totally present with that energy; just give yourself a while and be present with it. Now intensify the energy, and even more, and again be with it for a while, a minute or some minutes or even longer than that.

What changed?

I recommend that you write down what changed for you after being present with the energy of depression for a while. Do you notice that you have made that energy more powerful than you? It's just an energy. So how real is depression and how real have you made it by agreeing and aligning to the point of view that it is real?

What if depression is nothing but an interesting point of view?

Is the energy of depression a familiar energy for you, and is that the energy that you call your life? Have you defined this energy as who you are? Again, your point of view creates your reality. If you define the energy of depression as who you are, you are creating you as depressed. Say to yourself, "Interesting point of view, I have this point of view" again and again.

People who are so-called depressed usually pick up the sadness of other people and try to change it by taking it on and locking it into their bodies. Becoming aware of the fact that you are aware of other people's sadness can change a lot for you.

Depression does not have to look a certain way. Sometimes people look happy and seem happy, but they are not happy; they are actually sad and you are aware of that. How often have you made yourself wrong when people look happy and smile a lot, when you are aware that they are actually not happy, while thinking there must be something wrong with you for being aware of their unhappiness?

And how much do you then think that this unhappiness is yours, making yourself wrong for being unhappy in their presence when they are so seemingly "happy." You are just aware of what is really going on while looking at their faces that pretend to be happy. What if you are not the un-happy one?

You and your body pick up the unhappiness around you, and if you do not ask a question, you buy that unhap-piness as yours. You think it is you that is unhappy and you say to yourself that you are unhappy and then you look for evidence to prove that point of view as real like, "See, I am frowning which means that I am unhappy. See I have tears in my eyes, that means I am sad." You could ask, "Who does this belong to? Is it really me that is unhappy, or am I aware of somebody else's unhappiness?" Most of the time you are picking up other people's unhappiness, thinking and concluding that it is yours.

When I ask my clients, if they had somebody around them who was depressed and unhappy when they grew up, most of them say "yes" and some say "no." Asking more questions creates the awareness that there was indeed somebody who was unhappy but who looked and pretended to be happy. Acknowledging the fact that they had been aware of the unhappiness around them while growing up and the fact that it didn't belong to them lightens up their whole universe.

People spend their entire lives trying to make others happy by taking on their unhappiness and locking it into their bodies, making it theirs. How much are you doing that all the time with everybody? This is the energy you use to create your life? This has nothing to do with you or creating what you really would like. It is creating you through other people's realities. It is defending and saving other people's realities and not creating yours.

There is no need to judge yourself for doing that. How grateful can you be for now becoming aware of that? Knowing that this is what you are doing most of the time gives you the gift of choice. You can now, in every moment of your life, be aware of whether you are buying other people's realities as yours and healing them without them being interested in changing. You could also just be aware of what is going on around you, have no point of view about it, and start creating your life.

You have one problem. You are basically a happy person, but you are keeping that a secret from everybody, including yourself.

Being aware of other people's unhappiness and trying to heal it is not a limitation; it is a capacity you have. Acknowledge the greatness of you and how aware you are and your ability to be happy. Does that make you lighter? Remember what makes you lighter is true for you. Just because you can feel something does not make it real. You assume everything you are aware of is a feeling you have and that it is yours so you can be like everybody else, so you can be as unhappy as everybody else, so you can be normal. How fun is that?

Everything is a choice. Depression is a choice. If you are choosing to be depressed you are choosing it because it makes you happier than choosing to be happy.

I did not realize this for a long, long time. I tried to make it logical, except it is not logical. I always thought that I had to work through all my "problems" to be happy. I thought that happiness is something I get to have when I have solved all my problems and when I have figured out why I am unhappy, and when I understand the reasons for unhappiness. Except more and more problems showed up to solve, because I had decided that my job is to solve problems for myself and for others. Choosing that as my job, more problems showed up so I could keep my job. Now that is an interesting choice.

I am changing it now and asking myself, "How can I use what I am aware of as a source of joy? What else can I choose now that would change everything?"

Being unhappy and depressed is a choice and there is nothing wrong with that choice. It is something that works for the person for whatever reason. Acknowledging that it is a choice creates the space where you can change your choice anytime.

Happiness is the natural state you can choose, when you are not choosing against you.

Being happy is being you.

If you are being happy, you are the space where magic can show up, where everything and everyone can contribute to you. You are realizing that you cannot be alone. You are being the vibration that allows for more of you and more happiness to show up.

You might say that you don't know how to be happy or to change your life. It is not about the how. Choosing something different by making a demand that your life will change is what changes everything.

What about starting to demand of yourself to be and receive something greater right now?

You have choice in every moment

You are choosing in every moment. Be aware of the fact that you have a choice in everything you do, even if it is walking to your fridge and choosing to take out a coke. You do not have to choose—you get to choose. It is your privilege to choose. Choice is the creation of your reality. Start choosing in ten second increments. Now what are you choosing? Ten seconds are over. Now what are you choosing?

It is not about what is right to choose or best to choose. It is about choosing whatever it is. No choice is better than the other, they are just different choices. You have to do this in order to know what I am talking about.

Go out and choose. Smell a flower. Ten seconds are over, now what are you choosing—to continue smelling or something else? Do that for a while, so you become aware of the fact that you have choice and that everything you do and be is just a choice and not right or wrong. This allows you to come out of the place where you have decided that you do not have the capacity to choose. Choosing is creating and it creates the movement in your life that leads to more joy and everything you desire.

What energy, space and consciousness can you and your body be that allows you to be the joy of choice and creation you truly be?

Everything that does not allow that to show up will you destroy and uncreate it?

Thank you.

Right and wrong, good and bad, pod and poc, all nine, shorts boys and beyonds.

CHAPTER FOURTEEN

DEAD MAN WALKING

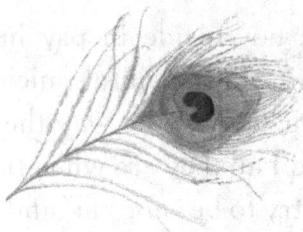

In psychiatry many people have thoughts about dying and taking their lives. Some of them attempt suicide. Psychiatry in Sweden has a so-called "zero tolerance for suicide" which means no suicide should occur and practitioners, whether they are doctors, therapists or social workers, should aim to make their patients not commit suicide. It is basically a point of view that suicide is wrong and that it is a failure as far as the patient and the practitioner are concerned. There are similar points of view about that in other countries.

Living in this world, working in psychiatry and looking at how people function, I have always wondered how much people are actually living. Most people exist, doing almost the same things on a daily basis as if they are on autopilot, as if that is all there is. Their bodies are tired, their heads are filled with judgments and conclusions.

What does that have to do with being alive? How much is that the energy of dying a slow death, a slow suicide? Having concluded what is possible and what is not possible and projecting that on the future, how many people are actually dead men walking? Where is the living; where is the adventure?

We talk about no suicide in psychiatry while people everywhere commit slow, painful suicide every day: the way they treat their bodies, the way they treat each other, they way they cut off all they are when they start a relationship, the way they try to be "normal" and the same as everybody else. They are concluding what is going to be instead of asking a question about what could be.

The people who attempt suicide are often those who take more action than the people all around us who just get by and exist, trying to be normal and trying to survive. Yes. Survive. How many people do you know who do more than survival and who do just enough to get by and not more?

You might get upset reading this as this perspective does not match this reality's point of view. What if there was no wrongness in anything? What if it was not wrong to just want to get by or to attempt suicide or to live?

What if it is about you becoming aware of what it is you are creating in your life and for you to choose what it is you really would like?

What if you would come out of dying into living and thriving?

Everything is the opposite of what it appears to be and nothing is the opposite of what it appears to be.

What are you choosing? Survival or thrival?

CHAPTER FIFTEEN

DO YOU REALLY WANT TO CHANGE?

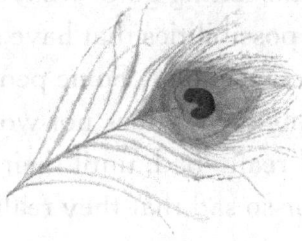

Now the part for the real brave ones.

How many times have you said that you want change, tried all kinds of techniques, and then after a short while ended up back in the same old ways and in the same old patterns? The question is, did you really ask for change or did you just want change?

"To want" means to lack, if you look it up in a dictionary prior to 1920. So did you really desire change and did you really choose change or did you want (lack) change?

I hear so many of my clients say they want change and most of them are not willing to have real change. Real change means something totally different, realizing the old way of doing things does not work, and being willing to embrace something totally different. Most people want a different version of the same old. There is absolutely no wrongness in that. This is the way we have been taught.

We have learned that things are the way they are; behaviors, relationships, people, yes everything in this reality is the way it is, and it is possible to change all that to a certain degree, but not more. We have never learned to ask for real change and for a different reality.

"Different" means letting go of what does not work and opening up to new possibilities that have not existed before. It is a choice. An active choice. Some people wait for a long time until they change what does not work for them. They wait until they feel really bad, until their bodies hurt, until they are so angry or so sad that they realize that something has to change.

Something has to change. That is the demand with which change starts. You are in charge. You are the steward of your own ship. Waiting for the lights to turn green or for somebody to do it for you takes a lot of waiting. Does that really work for you? Is waiting really your best talent and ability? Or is it time for you to ask for a different possibility?

Look at the people that get everything they desire. Do they say, "Oh, could I please maybe have that?" or are they demanding whatever they desire to show up? They are demanding it with their very being and always expecting it to show up. What would it take for you to choose to be the energy of demand and for you to choose to receive?

Yes. Receiving is a big part in that game. How much have you been brainwashed with the ideas that change takes a lot of time, is a lot of work, and that you are somebody who cannot have everything you desire? Are these your ideas or the points of view of the immutable (unchangeable) laws of this reality that you have been fed your whole life: everything is what it is, everything stays the same, and change is a threat.

What if there was nothing wrong with that, and what if it is just for you to acknowledge that this reality and your reality are different. What makes you feel lighter? The fact that everything stays the same with a slight variation, or that you can create and enjoy your reality as you desire where everything is changeable? What do you know?

I did not ask what you think, what your brain says. I asked what you know. What you know is much faster than your brain's capacity to process information. I ask for what you have always known was possible, but never allowed yourself to be because you have had people around you that told you it is not possible. Getting all those points of view out of your way—all the points of view from other people and this reality about how and why things are not possible —allows you for the first time in your life to receive. To receive what is truly possible for you.

Ask and you shall receive. Ask a question and allow yourself to receive. Ask the universe to show you what you are truly capable of. Ask for more ease and joy in your life. Ask for your money situation to change and ask what it takes. Ask for fun relationships, sex. Ask your body to change and enjoy it.

When we ask for something different, it shows up the way it shows up and when it shows up. It always shows up different than you think it will. If it would show up the way you think it *should*, it would not be a different possibility, it would just be a small change of something you already have in your life; it would be something that your brain can calculate and project onto the future. It would be like visualization, which means it can never be greater than your brain's capacity to imagine.

Asking for a different possibility means to ask for it and to let it go and allow the whole universe to contribute to you so it can show up even greater than you could ever imagine. Is that of interest to you?

The only thing that is required is to release all your points of view about how and when it should show up and to receive it when it shows up. I say receive it and I mean receive it. Many people judge what the universe gifts them as not good enough or not as they expected it to be. No expectations, no judgments or calculations allows you to receive for real.

Next part of the change recipe is to be grateful for however and whenever it shows up. Gratitude is being in total allowance of everything. When you are grateful, you do not judge. When you are grateful for a person, you allow them to be what they are without expecting them to change. When you are grateful for what you are receiving and when you are grateful for what you are creating, you are being the contribution for it to become greater. From that space of gratitude, from being grateful for what is, you can ask for more. Ask:

Now what else is possible?

How does it get even better than this?

CHAPTER SIXTEEN

BURN OUT OR BURN UP?

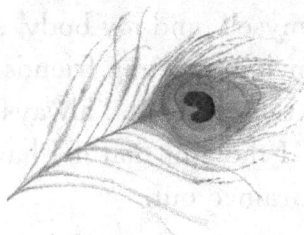

"Oh my god, I have so much to do, I am so stressed out, I think I am having a burn out." I hear so many people talking about how much they have to do and how little time they have doing everything they have decided they have to do, and how much that is stressing them and how bad they feel. Any of that sound familiar?

What we have learned is that there is a certain amount of things that one can do and if we do more than that we do too much, get tired and eventually get sick. Where the limit is, is different for everybody.

Where have you set your limit? How many projects can you have going on before you decide it is too much?

Is any of that real or is it the point of view people create, that tells them when it is enough?

Take myself as an example. I work as a clinical psychologist in psychiatry. I meet patients for private sessions;

I lead group sessions at the clinic, doing neuropsychological testing. At the same time, I run a full-time business that
includes travelling and facilitating one-to-five-day workshops. At the moment I do all the paperwork myself: web-
page, client contact, organizing, booking, accounting and
everything else that is part of a business. I also make time
for taking care of myself, and my body, enjoying exploring
different cities, dancing, meeting friends. The more I have
going on, the more relaxed I am. I always thought it was the
other way around. I thought that if I have a lot going on I
would be tired or drained out.

The times when I slowed myself down and tried to have
as much or little going on as other people, I was very tired
and frustrated.

Now, I always ask, "Who and what else can I add to my
life?" The more I add and the more projects I have going
on, the more energy I have. Why? Having a lot going on
matches my vibration and stimulates me to be creative.

How about you? Have you acknowledged what actually works for you and your body, or are you buying other
people's points of view about what is possible and what is
not possible?

Have you ever had a project where you were so inspired
that you were working with it all day long and forgot to
eat? You did not eat because your body did not require it.
Your body received the energy it needed from the energy
you generated when you were working with something that
was fun for you. It is like having a motor that runs and runs.
There is the point of view out there that this is dangerous. It
is not dangerous as long as you listen to yourself and your
body. As long as you know when it is time to keep on work-

ing, when it is time to go for a run or a walk in nature, when it is time to sleep and when it is time to eat.

Your body knows what it requires and it will tell you when you start asking it. What makes you feel light is right. There is nothing you can do wrong in this game. Start by choosing something and see how it goes, be aware of yourself, and then if it is light keep on; if it is not, then choose something else. Easy? Too easy?

Who and what else can you add to your life?

Being burned out is based on the idea that there is a lack of energy. There is no lack of energy, there are just points of view that do not allow you to access the energies that are available. Are you aware that your body has enough energy in the mitochondrial cells to operate a city the size of San Francisco for three months? That is how much energy you have available in your body. Yet you act as though you have to be tired all the time. Do you ever access all your energy?

Being tired and your energy being limited is a point of view that creates a limitation. What about asking your body when and how long it needs to sleep? It may be different every day, yet, we have learned that we always need 6–8 hours per night. And then people wonder why they wake up in the middle of the night not able to sleep. Well, what about asking if the body needs more sleep? If not, get up, read, write, enjoy the nighttime and its stillness. Great ideas can come at that time.

When everybody else is asleep, it is time to ask:

What would I like to generate and create as my future? What is truly possible for me that I have not acknowledged?

While other people are sleeping and their thoughts are quiet, it is easier for you to access what you are aware of as greater possibilities for you and your life. Ask:

What else would you like to create that makes your heart sing?

If there were no lack and no limits, what else would you like to add to your life? What if you would not have to choose either a family or a career, or this or that? What if you could have it all and make it work? What if you do not have to do it all by yourself? Who else can you add to your life that contributes to all the things you would like to create, and what if that would be a contribution to these people as well? Adding to your life adds energy, and you starting to choose will create the awareness of what works for you and what does not.

What energy, space and consciousness can you and your body be to be the creator source you truly be?

Everything that does not allow that to show up, will you destroy and uncreate it? Thank you.

Right and wrong, good and bad, pod and poc, all nine, shorts, boys and beyonds.

CHAPTER SEVENTEEN

RELATIONSHIP—KILLING YOU SOFTLY?

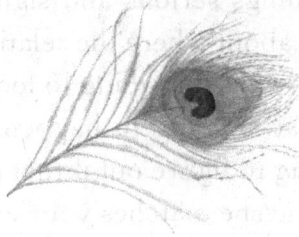

Ow do relationships work for you? If you are one of those lucky people who knows how to make relationships work for you, there is no need for you to read this section. If you are one of the other 99% and wonder if it is ever going to work for you, I recommend you read on.

Did you know that the definition of relationship is the distance between two objects?

Two people meet, both happy and inspired by one another, looking forward to something greater, butterflies in their stomach when they think of each other, happy when they get together, except.... Well you know.... How long does it usually last until you wonder what happened? Where is the joy? Where is that lightness that used to be there? Discussions begin, both parties fight to be right and make themselves and the other person wrong. Both try to make themselves fit into the box called relationship. Things start to go downhill. We have learned that this is a normal phase in relationships that are starting to get serious.

Funny how people call it "serious" relationships. Are we having relationships to be serious?

When things start to go downhill, this is the point at which you make things serious and significant and try to come to conclusion about where the relationship is heading, trying to figure out what it is going to look like and project into the future what is going to happen. Is this the point where you are trying to figure out if that person is the right one for you and if he/she matches your expectations?

Notice that when you read those last sentences that the light energy just disappeared. That is exactly what occurs when you start thinking, going into your head, figuring out and projecting into the future what is going to happen with this person. You separate from the joy you recently were being with each other. How much have you bought the point of view that this phase is normal and a part of the deal and that it is necessary? Is that true? Does that make you feel lighter? Whose point of view is that? Is that really your point of view? What else is possible?

The first question you can ask yourself to have more clarity in that area is, "Truth, do I really desire a relationship?" Have you ever asked yourself that question? Or have you assumed that you would like to have a relationship? How much have you entrained to the point of view that you are supposed to have one because everybody else has the same point of view and is trying to make it work? Do you have the necessity of having a relationship? Everywhere we have a necessity of anything, we have to somehow fight against it at the same time we are trying to achieve it. Where is the choice? What is it that you truly would like?

What is a relationship for you? Who would you like to have a relationship with who actually would be a contribution to your life? How would that relationship look? What exactly do you expect from the other person? What exactly does the other person expect from you? Most relationships are based on common insanity. Harsh words? Well look around. How many relationships do you see where both parties are really happy; where they are being themselves and where having each other contributes to their lives expanding? Not so many?

Most people cut off the best of themselves, the very thing that the other person was attracted to in the first place, to fit in the box of relationship and to be able to exist together. Is that enough for you or are you desiring more? What if you could choose how you would like to create your relationship?

Instead of drowning in the fantasy that someday it all will work out and your partner will understand you and be and do what you would like, you could start today with a total relationship makeover. How? By asking yourself, "So, which part of this relationship actually works for me and which part does not?" The parts that don't work, ask if you can change, and if so, how you can change them.

When you renovate your house, you do the same—you walk around and check out all the parts and pieces of your house to see what you would like to keep and what not keep, and where it needs to be refreshed. Now having another person involved besides you means that they also get to choose what they would like to change or not. If you would like to change something and they are not interested, it is up to you to be in allowance of that and ask yourself if you can live with that.

Ask questions so you can get all the information to know what exactly you would like as a relationship and ask your partner what works for him/her. Then ask yourself if the way the other person would like to have the relationship actually works for you. Do not expect the other person to change or to desire the same as you. That is being pragmatic.

I have a friend who is married, and in the bedroom her husband has a big cozy cushion that he likes to lie on and he never puts that cushion away. He leaves it right in front of the bed. Many times my friend has fallen over the cushion during the night when she gets up to use the toilet. She has asked her husband a thousand times to please remember to put away the cushion before they go to bed and her husband usually forgets. This has gone on for years.

After many of those years, she learned not to bother about it anymore and trusts that her husband will not put away the cushion. She knows this is something he will not change and she is in allowance of that, so she asked the question about how to make it work for her. She realized that instead of being angry or creating the point of view that her husband does not care about her, she just remembers to put away the cushion herself.

What is a great relationship? Where you get to be you. A great relationship is where both partners are in allowance of themselves and each other. Where you and the other person do not look for the other person to fulfill their needs. Where you let the other person be and do whatever they desire and where they let you do and be whatever you be and desire.

Notice the part about being and doing what you desire. Do you even know what you desire in life? Or are you looking for an answer in the other person? How is that working for you?

A great relationship starts with you. Trusting you, honoring you, being in allowance of you, being grateful for you, being vulnerable. Vulnerable means having no barriers up to receiving, not defending you, being you. You can have a sense of that when you lie in the grass until you no longer sense a separation between you and the earth, where you receive the contribution every single molecule is wishing to be for you. Yes, every molecule is wishing to contribute to you and the only thing you have to do is to receive it.

Most people would rather wait for the right person to show up and have already decided how that person should contribute to them. What about receiving the whole universe instead of one person? What about receiving contribution as it comes without having a point of view how it shows up? What if with every person no matter what they do or say you could ask:

What gift is this person to me that I have not acknowledged? What contribution can this person, this situation be to me and my body?

What would be possible for you then?

◇ ◇ ◇

When it's time to move on

At this point in the book, are you getting more aware of how much you have been buying into the wrongness of you your whole live? All the labels—depression, anxiety, personality disorder—are ways of describing how wrong you are. These are conclusions that convince you there is something wrong with you and that you are not part of the "A team," the "sane" people. (I always wondered where these people are. Where are the people who are sane and normal? If you meet any, please let me know. So far I have only met people who are desperately trying to be normal and are doing everything to fit in.)

Are you aware of how much you are controlling yourself to not step outside the box, to not dance to a different rhythm, your rhythm? And how much are you controlling your body and being; how much living are you turning off? No wonder people are getting depressed by the amount of energy they are suppressing and controlling in their being and body. No wonder people are creating pain and suffering and tension in their muscles. If you spend your whole life working hard not being you, and even harder to fit into what has been handed to you as this reality, you are certain to go crazy.

How much of your insanity are you creating as an attempt to be normal?

What? I know it does not make logical sense. I am telling you insanity and mental illness are not even a bit logical. The majority of people's pain and suffering is not cognitive or logical; it is created at some point for some reason that people do not remember. And it is not even relevant why they are suffering. Many modalities look for the cause as though that would change the problem.

Has it ever changed anything for you to find out why you are suffering? To look for the reason is to look for what is wrong in your head, your mind. And what created the problem in the first place? Yes, your thinking, your cognitions, your mind. So trying to figure out why you have a problem is trying to look for the solution at the same place where you created it. Interesting. This is where people lose themselves in their own heads.

If you would not think yourself out of your problem, what would you be aware of?

Who created the problem? When you start to acknowledge that it is actually you who created the problem, you have the chance to choose again. Isn't that great news? You created the problem in the first place, which means that you are the one who can uncreate it. So if you would not buy into the wrongness of you, if you would not think that you are weak and pathetic, what potency of change would you be aware of?

What are you actually capable of that you have not yet acknowledged?

What if you could change anything in your life? Anything? Start by asking. Choose one area of your life and ask, "Universe what would it take for this change and be greater and more ease than I could ever imagine?" What if your job was simply to ask and allow the universe to contribute to you. Easy? Yes.

So how much of your insanity and mental illness have you created to fit into this reality? Mental illness and insanity are creations, they are not real. It means that you do not fit the norm and it means that you not fitting the norm is wrong. So, to at least fit in a little bit you create yourself as mentally insane. So who are you truly that you have never acknowledged?

What if instead of dwelling on the past and being sad about how you were treated, you could treat you as you should have been treated? What if you were your own dream partner, how would you treat yourself? What if you would be your own best lover, what would you choose?

CHAPTER EIGHTEEN

HAPPINESS IS JUST A CHOICE

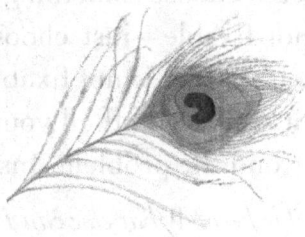

This chapter title might be provoking if you've been convinced that happiness is just available for some very privileged people on this planet and that you're not one of those happy VIPs. Have you decided that happiness is not a choice you have? How many reasons and justifications do you have convincing yourself that happiness is not possible for you? "My childhood, my parents, my body, my money situation, my this and that...." What have you decided that keeps you from being happy?

What if happiness is a *choice* you have available? What if you can demand of yourself:

No matter what my past was, no matter who I decided I am, I will let this go now and open the door to more of me, to the happiness I truly be.

Whenever something comes up in your life that is not light, choose again. Yes. Just choose again and redirect.

Put "happiness" in your personal GPS and take the next road to get you there.

We have learned to fix problems, to deal with problems and to solve them. What about asking a question instead like, "Can I change this?" If you get a no on that, redirect and take another road, choose something else that is lighter. Why fix what is not fixable—just choose something else. When you fix a problem that is not fixable you get stuck in it, lose yourself in it, and turn off all your awareness about what is possible beyond the problem. Instead ask:

What else is possible here? What else can I choose that keeps me moving forward?

Whatever presents itself as light and a different possibility that matches the energy of what you would rather desire, choose that. Yes, this is shamelessly easy. How much of your life have you spent fixing your problems and those of others? And what was the effect of that? Did it create what you desired or did it take you further down the rabbit hole? How many times have you done that routine? Is it time for a new routine? Why continue with what does not work instead of trying something completely different, even if most people would call it crazy and wrong? Do what works for you.

Scan through your life and look at all the times when you chose something that was right for you even though people around you had the point of view that it was totally crazy and wrong. Did that choice make your life bigger and better or smaller and worse?

Choosing what is right for you, what makes you light and lightens up your universe will expand your life as it matches the vibration of who you truly are as a being. It matches what you would like to create. You are conscious-ness embodied. The vibration that you truly are is light and joyful and peaceful. Everything else is the limitations that you have made real. Real is only what you make real and what you agree and align with or resist and react to.

Being happy is a choice you have available all the time.

Have you noticed that the only times you have a prob-lem is when you do not acknowledge your potency to change what is going on? Do you make yourself less potent than you truly are and agree to the fact that you have a problem and that you cannot change it? Asking a question will change that immediately.

What other choices and possibilities are available for you? That question alone opens up a new door where you thought that there was no door. It gives you an awareness of something different. It is not about getting a picture and a word or sentence of what that other thing is. It gives you a sense that there is something else. An awareness of an energy probably beyond words. The only thing you have to do is choose whatever matches that energy to create some-thing different in your life.

Do it. The more you do it the easier it will become for you. There is nothing you can do wrong.

People usually have a certain area in their lives where they perceive themselves as stuck: their finances, relation-ship, body, business. What is the area in your life where you have decided that you have a problem that you cannot change? When you decide that you have a problem you then go and look for evidence to support that you have a problem. You look for justifications to make your problem real and solid. It is like cementing in what you have decided is your problem and then adding bricks every time you agree to the point of view that you have a problem.

If you decide that you have money problems, every time you look at your bank account you say, "Oh my god, I have so little money, I will not be able to pay my bills." If you decide you have problems with your partner you will go, "See, he did not take out the trash again, he really does not care for me." If you decide that you have problems with your body, you go look for what is wrong with your body. These are all the places where you do not ask questions and decide there is a problem and then convince yourself that it indeed is a problem that is not changeable.

The areas that people call their problem areas are exactly the places where they do not ask questions. So which areas of your life do you not ask questions about and have already decided that all is hopeless? What if you started to ask questions with everything that is not light and not the way you desire it to be?

Ask the four questions:

What is it?

What do I do with it?

Can I change it?

How can I change it?

Those four questions can change any situation. It is not about finding the answer to these questions. It is about opening up to more awareness so you can look from a different perspective on the situation you are in. Instead of coming to a conclusion like, "I am so stuck, I am so bad, I feel so sad," ask what it is, if you can change it, and how you can change it.

After asking if you can change it, sometimes you will get a no. That allows you to have more peace and be relaxed; knowing that you can just let it be what it is and you can stop working so hard trying to change what is not change-able at the moment.

When I work with clients I have those four questions with me all the time. The clients tell me their problems and in my head I ask, "What is it? What do we do with it? Can we change it? How can we change it?" After every ques-tion, I wait for the awareness. Awareness is not an answer; it is an energy, like a door that opens that allows me to know where to go next.

What if life was not about coping with problems and having tolerance for suffering but about enjoying living and enjoying being you? How much more could you generate and create if you were the joy of you? How much more ease would you have?

Are you willing to have that? Are you willing to say goodbye to the old paradigm of problem solver and toler-ater of crap and be the terminator of crap? (I just could not resist that wordplay!) What if you added a new routine—to enjoy your life and choose what is the light routine?

It's ok to be happy. You can just sit there and swing.

CHAPTER NINETEEN

DOES THE MAJORITY REALLY RULE?

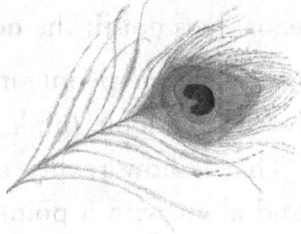

L et's look at a concept that is a big part of this reality: Majority rules. It means that a numerical majority of a group holds the power to make decisions binding on all in the group. Let's revisit the world of diagnosis, which is a big part of healthcare. The practitioner is obliged to diagnose every patient that comes for a visit. Their symptoms are categorized into boxes with names, so-called diagnoses.

What are these boxes, these diagnoses, based on? The whole system of categorizing is based on the idea that majority rules. The way the majority of the population lives and behaves and thinks and feels is considered normal. This is the so-called norm to which the rest is compared to.

Comparison is based on judgment. You look at a person and you judge whether they fit within the norm or not. Then the conclusion is formed. This is an equation that is part of most people's lives all the time. You walk into a café and you look around for a place where you would like to sit based on the information you get about the people sitting in the cafe, how they look, how they act, if they sit alone or not, and you form judgments and conclusions about what you are aware of and whether the people fit into the norm or not. Nobody wants to sit next to somebody who seems strange—which means does not fit the norm.

Everywhere and every time people interact, they judge others and themselves to act, look, think and feel according to what is normal. That is how reality is created. At least two people agree and align with a point of view and they create that as real and it becomes their reality. They create that point of view as solid enough to use it as a reference point to judge other points of view as right or wrong. The more solid it is, the more real people see it. And it becomes "the thing." Whatever "the thing" is, it becomes more real than anything else. It becomes the guideline, the standard. Anything else that does not fit the standard cannot even come into people's awareness as it is too different. It sits there like a huge elephant. This is the creation of limitation.

Looking for a place to sit in the café, you will focus on the people that meet the standard, the normal ones. What if there are people that do not fit the norm, but sitting next to them and talking with them would inspire you and change your world?

Many people who are looking for a partner usually look for the same person they have been in relationship before just in a different body, because these people fit their standards. It is familiar. They create the same problems over and over as they try to maintain the kind of life they have judged to be normal.

What have you judged as normal that maintains your limitations?

Everything that is will you destroy and uncreate it? Thank you.

Right and wrong, good and bad, pod and poc, all nine, shorts, boys and beyonds.

What if you could be the question that allows you to perceive greater possibilities at all times?

Notice how that last question was way lighter than the first part of this chapter? Once again, what makes you light is right. Easy. What if you could ask a question every time you or somebody else presented their "thing" for you and it makes you feel so heavy. Ask: "What is the lie here, spoken or unspoken?" As soon as you spot the lie, it no longer sticks on you and you are free. You no longer think about it.

Majority rules. Heavy or light? What if majority rules just was an interesting point of view? Not right nor wrong, nothing to react against or resist to or agree or align with, just an interesting point of view.

I was in a store the other day to buy some lingerie and I took a piece that was in the size I usually wear. I looked at it and figured, "Hmmm, that is kind of big for being my size, what is up with that?" The salesperson looked at me and replied to my nonverbal question, "This is not your size, Madame. Pick the smaller one, we just changed all our clothes to fit European standards which means that everybody has gone down one size."

How funny is that? The whole clothing standard and size has changed because most people have become bigger and now we have a new standard. I used to be a medium and now I am no longer average; now I am below average.

How is that for funny. And kind of smart. So many people feeling even better about themselves if they have gone down one size without doing anything. Sure is a great way to get people to shop more.

It is all just an interesting point of view and not real. Everything can change.

What is normal and not normal in this reality is based on normal distribution which is dictated by the majority. In the bell curve, 68% are in the middle and are what is considered normal and average and the rest are either below or above. What people do is try to find their place in this reality in regards to where the majority is functioning from. Some people place themselves in the middle where the majority are and some choose to be greater and some choose to be lesser. Yes, there is a choice.

Where are you placing yourself in the scheme of this reality? Are you placing yourself where the majority is or are you making yourself lesser or greater?

Look at the different areas of your life and where you place yourself in those areas. Maybe you allow yourself to be greater than most people in the area of relationship and less than most in the area of money. Or the other way around.

I invite you to become aware that people constantly compute and calculate what is normal to have and be. How much money is normal and average to have; how much success in business is normal to have; how many children, and so on, and then they calculate where they would like to be in relation to the ideals of this reality. How much choice does that allow? Not so much. Have you ever asked what you would like to be and create as your life that may not fit the ideals of this reality?

What makes you happy that may not be normal?

If you spend your life trying to fit in and being normal you will never know what makes you happy. What if you and your reality were way beyond even the maximization of this reality? Way off the scale. How much choice and access to the greatness of you would you have then?

Finding your place in reality with mental illness

Mental illness is a way of placing oneself on the below average part of the bell curve, but still within the curve of normality. Mental illness is a way of fitting in, a way of finding one's place in this reality. It creates a confictual universe where one enjoys being different but is not willing to be too different and creates a resistance against being too different and a reason and justification to still fit in.

The resistance of being totally different and forcing oneself to fit in creates a lot of suffering and psychological and physiological pain. People with mental illness have a way of defending this reality and a way of defending what people think they are.

For example, ADHD, OCD, autism and bipolar are ways of deviating as much as possible from the place the majority functions from without turning totally insane. These are choices people make to give the impression that they are disabled. In fact, acknowledging and receiving their capacities would allow them to go beyond the scale and be and receive the greatness they truly are.

To make mental illness real, how much of your awareness do you have to cut off to agree and align with that point of view? Interesting that people assume that because many people behave a certain way that it is right. How much energy do you use on a daily basis to make that a reality for you?

Get that energy, right now. Connect to your body by taking a deep breath and let it go from your head down to your toes, and get the energy you lock into your body to make you normal. Now ask:

What energy, space, and consciousness can me and my body be to use that energy to be me and to create my life?

Now that you asked that question, perceive the energy. Is it different? There is no right way for you to feel. Just allow it to change your world. You might need to give up your need to control your life and yourself. Letting go of control, what does your body say about that? Do you hear it cheering?

What if being out of control is the way you gain total control? Being out of control means being totally aware and receiving all information at all times. It allows you to know what step to take and when to create your reality, as you no longer try to figure out with your brain what is right and wrong and good and bad. Ask:

What would it take for me to be totally out of control, out of form, structure and significance?

This is the place where you can be everything and create yourself new and different all the time. Total choice. Fun?

What grand and glorious adventures are waiting for you?

CHAPTER TWENTY

"SPACE PHOBIA"— DO YOU AVOID SPACE?

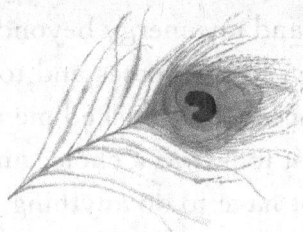

I had some fun the other day as I have every day. I was in my apartment and I had nothing specific planned, and as I sat there I became aware that there really was nowhere I had to go. There was no need in my world to do anything or to meet anybody. No need to get some delicious food. Not even the need to fill the space with thoughts. Just space and no need.

The awareness came up for me, "Wow, how much is that the space that most people avoid. The space people fill with thoughts, feelings, sex, relationship or something to do?" This space is too uncomfortable for most people as there is no necessity; no standard or reference point telling you where to go and what to do. The space of total choice. The space where you get to create what you truly would like.

Just for fun I came up with the name "space phobia." The space that most people avoid like the plague in what-

ever way they can to a degree that they are phobic about
being that space.

Another day I was at a horse festival and it was so
crowded I could sense the irritation that came up for everybody with so many people being in one place. I knew I had
the choice to drown in that irritation and become irritated
myself, or to be the space where the irritation did not affect
me. I chose to expand my energy beyond the festival as big
as possible, connect to the horses and to nature, the earth,
the trees and the ocean, and I asked me and my body to be
that vibration. All it took was a choice and to ask to be that
vibration. I did not have to do anything special or perform
a ritual to get to be that space. I just connected.

What showed up was that everything started to be
peaceful and at ease. I was simply aware of the vibration
that got created with other's thoughts and their points of
view and I was being totally calm about it. And after a while
I knew it was time for me to go.

Interesting thing was that I perceived so many of the
people's bodies wanting to go somewhere else except they
did not listen. They had decided that they had to stay at the
festival for whatever amount of time they had decided was
right. All these people, with their thoughts and feelings, had
created a solidity they call reality which they are comfortable with, as it is familiar to them. They would rather stay
in the place of familiarity being irritated than listen to their
bodies tell them what else was possible to have more ease.
Even though their bodies were screaming and asking them
to go somewhere else, they could not hear that due to everything they had decided already.

This is an example of where people do everything they
can to not be the space they actually truly are. They have

an addiction of filling the space they are with the polarity of thoughts and feelings and things to do and people to meet and relationships to create and business to be made.

Another example is the drama and trauma people create where soap operas pale in comparison. Where people pick fights or make themselves the victims to create the drama that creates enough entertainment to not be bored.

I have a friend who is this brilliant, caring and potent being and as soon as he started to be that space he truly is and every time he was on the verge of creating a phenomenal life, he chose to either start a relationship with a woman that brought him back to being where he was before, or he allowed his ex-wife to torture him and make him wrong for being successful. He did not create his relationships to expand and contribute to being the brilliance he is. No, he chose to make the woman the answer and a reference point to not lose touch with this reality, to be controlled and to make sure he is not alone.

Can an infinite being ever be alone? That lie is what makes so many people go into relationships that do not work for them. They would rather have a bad relationship than none at all. Say what?

What are you using to keep you anchored in this reality and what is real and normal? Who and what are you using to control you so you never show up as the brilliance of you? Who or what is your eternal jailor, keeping you imprisoned for all eternity?

Is now the time to destroy and uncreate everything you have created to keep that in place? Just say "yes" to yourself if you choose to change it. That is all it takes.

What is possible beyond that? The space beyond thoughts, feelings, emotions, points of view, conclusions, projections, expectations, judgments, rejections and separations. These are all the things you use to make yourself feel like others. Being space has no value in this reality as you cannot cognitize it or describe it. The space you truly are and already are is where you get to be you, like the ocean, the sun, the earth and the animals. The space where you are the question, the choice, the possibility, the contribution and where you get to create you. Where you can create your life, your business, your friendships, your money, the way you truly desire.

How?

Ask for it and then allow it to show up when it shows up and the way it shows up. "What would it take for me to have more money than I can ever spend?" And receive the information about what it takes for you to create it. Don't hurry. Don't conclude that it does not show up just because it did not show up yesterday. Ask that question for whatever you would like to create:

What would it take for...to show up?

Being the space of you is where you do not make any point of view or judgment real or significant anymore. You receive everything and judge nothing. You are not the effect of anything as you allow everything to come to you with ease and joy and glory, and you allow it all to contribute to you, your body and your life. Being that space makes you the catalyst for a totally different world. By being in total allowance, people around you are not able to hold on to their fixed points of view. They melt in your presence. Everything that is an invention like thoughts, feelings and emotions, judgments and points of view dissipate in your presence. And that invites the people around you to choose.

All of life comes to you with ease and joy and glory!™

This is a mantra you can use to receive everything in life with ease and joy and glory, the good and the bad. Say this ten times in the morning and then times in the evening and ease will come your way!

CHAPTER TWENTY-ONE

BEWARE OF SO-CALLED EX-PERTS

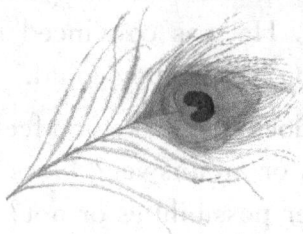

T here are many experts in this reality. Experts are people who have the role of being the one who has the answers. Usually experts have credentials, academic or otherwise. Doctors, therapists, psychologists, social workers and consultants are some of the experts in this reality.

Being an expert is something that is rarely questioned. People claim to be experts in all kinds of areas. They are experts because they say they are, not because they know better. Many experts, especially if they call themselves experts, tell their clients how what they have been doing so far is not working, and that they as experts have the answer and the solution.

Looking at experts for answers is how you make somebody else's points of view more valuable than what you know. You stop listening to yourself in favor of the expert's point of view. You judge yourself whether you are doing the right thing or the wrong thing. This is where you try to find out what you should do that makes you right so you can avoid being wrong. Does this create any freedom for you? Does this create what truly works for you?

* * *

On one of my travels I talked to a physicist who sees a lot of patients who smoke excessively and whose lungs are severely damaged. He was convinced that most of them would quit smoking if only they could.

Hearing that, does that make you feel light or heavy? Is that an awareness or an answer? Does that point of view open up for greater possibilities or not? How much is that doctor buying into the lies about his patients wanting to quit smoking just because they say so? And how much do you think he is finding evidence on a daily basis that his point of view is right? Every patient who says they would like to quit smoking but can't is making his point of view stronger, convincing him that people have a hard time stopping smoking. By buying those points of view, he is feeding his patients answers back to them, convincing them of their own point of view. This has nothing to do with empowerment.

I am not saying this doctor is wrong. I am inviting you to see this is something that is going on all the time in this reality.

People feed themselves and each other with lies, going further and further down the rabbit hole of their suffering without ever asking a question. What if you could use questions to empower yourself and others? What about being honest and really asking yourself:

Truth, would I really like to change this, would I really like to have a different possibility than the suffering I am choosing?

If you get a "no," great. Then you know what your point of view is in that moment. You know that you do not truly desire to change anything and you can stop trying so hard to change something when you are not interested in any change. This is like your right hand fighting your left hand and all you get is more pain. There is nothing bad or wrong with not wanting to change anything. It is just a choice. When you realize that you are not interested in change, you open up the door to even more choice. You can ask yourself:

Does not wanting to change work for me? What is the value of holding on to my pain and suffering?

Whatever comes up, you do not need to be able to put words to it. Just ask yourself: "Whatever comes up here by asking these questions, will I destroy and uncreate it all?" If it is a "yes" for you, use the clearing statement to dissipate the limitation.

Right and wrong, good and bad, pod and poc, all nine, shorts, boys and beyonds.

I recommend doing this many times as each repetition clears another layer of limitations.

Why people do not desire to change does not make sense since there is a lot of suffering involved. If it were logical and understandable there would be no problems in this world. We would have figured out the solutions a long time ago.

Many people wait quite long and suffer a lot before they choose something different. There is nothing wrong with that. Sometimes the self-torture has to hurt hard enough for people to demand something different. "No, I do not desire to change" can easily turn into "Yes, I am choosing to change." What is required is for you to first become aware of the "no" before you can get to the "yes." Once you choose "yes" it is way easier than you think to change.

Ninety percent of what it takes to change to something greater is the choice to demand, "Yes, I am changing this now, doing whatever it takes." Do not expect things to be different in the next second. Give it some time. By demanding of yourself to have something greater, you've already opened the door and the rest will follow. If it takes longer than you might like, do not give up, do not come to a conclusion that it does not work. You coming to a conclusion that it does not work stops what you just started to create. Keep on asking for something greater and choose what makes your life easier. You have everything it takes to create what you truly desire. There is nothing and no one that can stop you unless you let them.

Everything is the opposite of what it appears to be, and nothing is the opposite of what it appears to be

The example with the doctor is how experts can use their role to give people the answer they think is right, without being willing to see what is going on or asking questions that create something different. Empowering people, whether you have the role of an expert or not, is way easier than you might think it is. You can be dumb as dirt to empower people to be who they truly are.

Everything is the opposite of what it appears to be and nothing is the opposite of what it appears to be. Dumb or brilliant?

Empowering people is easy and fun. How come? You do not have to have any answers; you ask people questions to facilitate them to find out what is true for them. As an expert you have the answers ready and those answers are more important than anything else. Every time you go to a doctor, do you ask you and your body what it requires, or do you rely on the doctor to have the right answer for you?

How does the doctor know better? He might have more information than you on the matter, but that does not mean that he knows better. You could receive the expert's information and ask yourself and your body, "Truth, what do I know about this? What would work for me? What makes my life easier? Body, what do you require?"

You know. The more you ask yourself, the easier it will be for you to know. It is like building a muscle. Every time you rely on someone or something else you give away your power and make you the effect of someone else's point of view. That is a huge disservice to you and the world. What you know is a gift to the world.

There are many experts who are convinced that people do not know. They hold the point of view that they are too sick to know, that they are too diseased to know, that they are too handicapped to know. Nobody and nothing can ever take away your knowing. It is who you be. Nothing can take away who you be. No sickness, no person, nothing. What you know and be can be clouded and hard to access when people have diseases, take drugs, or are labelled "mentally ill." You can choose to be who you be and know that you know.

As an expert you can choose to make your education the valuable product, or you can use your role to empower people to know that they know.

Being useless

Therapists often ask me what approach I take when I hold sessions with clients. My approach is, before I start a session, I ask the question, "How useless can I be here?"

For many experts that triggers laughter or an open mouth. "What do you mean by 'useless'? Do you start with being useful and then go to useless? How does that work?"

I start with being useless and continue being useless.

What we learned as experts is to be useful; we are supposed to fix and handle the problem, have the right answer, the solution, and do what is right and what saves the client. How well does that work? Experts take on a lot of responsibility. How fun is it to have that kind of responsibility on you? Yes fun. Why are you doing your work? To suffer or to have fun? I know fun is not allowed in serious fields of experts.

It is for me. I break the serious rule. What about you?

Being responsible for the outcome of your work when it involves another person puts a lot of pressure on the expert. It is not the smartest choice. If you are getting angry now with this conversation, you might want to look at that for yourself.

What are you resisting to be and choose that if you would be it and choose it would expand your practice and your life beyond what you thought possible?

What freedom could you grant yourself that would expand your whole life? If you make yourself responsible for what another person chooses, or are vested in the outcome that the client has to get better, you might notice that your work gets quite hard. And the question is: "Is this empowering the other person?" Are you giving them the space to choose for themselves?

I used to think that I had to fix everybody, make them happy and that the goal of my sessions was to make people more sane and get them over their problems. I was tired and drained of energy by the end of my workdays and on the weekends I mostly slept. I knew this had to change.

I started to realize that it is not my responsibility whether people choose to change or not. I can give them the tools, the information and processes to let them know that they have choice. What they then choose is up to them. That is the greatest care and empowerment—to let people choose what they need to choose without having a point of view. I am not their savior or need to think I should help them. I can empower them to where they know that they have choice.

Being useless when I meet clients creates the space where people can explore where they are and what they would like to choose. It is where I do not come with any answers or points of view where the session should go or what we should cover or what the outcome should be. It takes me out of having to have the answers and proving that I am being useful which creates a relaxation in me and the client.

Have you ever had a session with an expert who desperately tried to give you the answers, make you change, convince you that his method would save you? How was that? I know I have been an expert like that every time I thought I knew better than my client and I know how contractive it was for me and the client. It led nowhere and the result was that I felt like a failure, and probably the client did too.

Most therapists are vested in the outcome about what the client should get out of the session and that their life should change. What if it is up to the client to change or not? Letting go of being vested in the outcome as a therapist creates more ease for the therapist and the client. Clients know when therapists want them to change and how. They have a sixth sense for that and it makes them work harder than they have to in order to be what the therapist wants them to be, instead of allowing it to be easy. Or the client resists and reacts to the therapist and stops the change that is possible.

What if a therapist simply provides the tools and the client chooses if, how and when to apply them?

Being useless allows me and my body to relax and ask the questions that unlock the client's awareness. It is having no point of view about anything, enjoying facilitating with no vestment in the outcome, being the space for possibilities to show up and allowing the client and me to be surprised about what is truly possible beyond the invention of limitation. It creates lightness and ease as we are both in exploration mode. Many "aha moments" show up and the client gets to learn to trust their knowing and to not rely on me.

Sexualness

Where does sexualness come into this conversation? Sexualness is a big part of being, creating and facilitating change.

Sexualness is the healing, nurturing, expansive, orgasmic and joyful energy that infuses our bodies. It is our natural way of being. Children are very familiar with this energy. They are highly sexual beings. They come in enjoying themselves and their bodies, always on the lookout for what and who they can play with. They are full of energy, and when they are tired they crash wherever they are and sleep. Whatever they choose in their play contributes to more play and more energy.

Have you decided you cannot be that anymore now that you are an adult?

Is that true? Or can you be that and express it in a way that works for you?

Being sexual is where you invite change and different possibilities into your life. Have you ever forced something into existence? You know how that feels. Forcing yourself to write an essay, making yourself create more money to pay the bills, forcing your partner to talk about something you have decided is important…you know what I am talking about. It takes a lot of energy and usually is very frustrating.

What about inviting sexualness to the party?

If you would treat everything and everyone as your lover, would you invite them to come?

And they will come. Treating everything and everyone like your lover also involves gratitude when they come so they are invited and motivated to future invitations. What if you would treat your money like your lover. Get that energy. More fun? Would that create more ease with money? What if you would treat your body like your lover? How much more fun could you have?

Have you ever forced your body to lose weight? How well did that work? What about being grateful for you and your body and inviting you and your body to change and ask what is possible: "Body, show me, how would you like to look?" You might be surprised what it shows you.

What can you choose on a daily basis that allows you and your body to be the energy of sexualness? What expands the healing, nurturing, expansive, orgasmic and joyful energy in your life and body? Taking a walk at the beach, dancing, writing, talking to a friend, having a bath? What is it for you? What if you would do that at least half an hour every day? How much would that create the energy of possibilities and living for all areas of your life?

I used to be one of those super-efficient people with long to-do lists that I would work through every day. I had the point of view that this is how things got done. I was frustrated, rushing through my days to accomplish everything on the list. Do you get the energy when you read this? It's not so fun, is it? I would get the things on my list done, but my life did not change. I thought that if I did it all it would eventually make my life better. It never did.

Add to that matter that I am OCD, which means that when I do something, I do it in every detail, which creates even more work. I realized that this is not the way I wish to create my life so I demanded myself to change it. I now start my day by asking what is the energy I would like my life to be. I become aware of the ease and the joy, the orgasmic, always expanding, nurturing, healing, fun energy I am asking for, and every morning I ask me and my body to be that energy, to sense it in every cell of my body. Being that energy I ask:

What can I choose today? Where can I put my energy today that allows me to generate and create my life greater than I thought was possible?

I choose what matches the energy of the life and living I am desiring. Sometimes it is taking a walk at the beach, sometimes it is talking to somebody who gives me information and inspiration to create something new.... Choosing that which contributes to my life and living creates a constant forward movement. I ask myself again and again, "What I can I choose now that expands my life?" and I choose again. That is being the question, the choice, the possibility and the contribution. The elements of expansion.

What if you choose for you and your body to be the energy of sexualness? What would be possible for you?

Sexualness is being like nature—vibrant and living. Nature is this grand orchestra that plays with the trees, the wind, sun, clouds, ocean, earth in the grandest of symphonies. It knows when it is time to change and institutes change with ease.

Having that ease with being and change, would you ever have a problem again?

Being sexual when you facilitate a client invites them to embody that energy. What about not cutting it off again? Sexualness does not imply having sex with people. It is being the energy that invites you and the other person to play again, to have ease with change and to let go of fixed points of view that create pain and suffering.

People always assume that being sexual means having sex and so they only allow themselves to be that energy in the bedroom. What about taking it out of the bedroom and into your whole life? What about letting the energy of sexualness permeate your whole reality? Being joyful, nurturing, caring, orgasmic, healing and expansive dissipates the separation you create with yourself and other people. It is not any more about the dynamic of expert/teacher and the patient. It is about you being you and inviting the other person to be themself.

Just being you creates change

What became clear to me as I worked with clients facilitating change is that the technique and the modality I work with is not the source of the change in the client.

Most therapists have the point of view their technique does the trick. With most modalities there is a certain way, a form and a structure in which it should be done. The therapist usually applies the technique and tries to do it right, spending a lot of time and energy. There are standards and reference points with which they compare their own work, and then they judge whether they have done it right or wrong and whether they have succeeded and achieved the result that they desired.

I have worked that way too. I read many books and attended seminars about many different ways of doing psychotherapy. I would find myself in constant judgment, having the point of view that I did not do it well enough, that I should have instead said this and that, or that the client did not get the change he or she was supposed to get. I would feel so bad and like a failure.

The books I read about therapy techniques would have those perfect examples on how therapy was conducted and how the therapist knew exactly what to say in the right moment that displayed how perfectly he was using the technique. In my sessions I tried to do the same; while I was with my client I would recall what I read in the books and what the therapist in the book said, and I tried to do it the same way or at least "correctly" enough, which never worked out quite well. My clients never said what the clients in the book said; they would just look at me funny and I would just feel worse. Welcome to a therapist's self-torture.

After one year of doing it the way I was "supposed to," I just could not do it anymore. I knew I had to change my way of working. Enough with the self-torture. Somewhere I had the awareness that there is a different possibility that allows working with clients to be way more ease and joy.

How?

I started to ask questions. I let go of all my points of view that there is a technique that creates change. I asked my clients what it is that helps them and what it is that creates change for them in the work we do. All of the people I asked said that it is me, the being I be—not what I say, but the caring I have for them, the way I listen and talk without judgment; that is the thing that changes them the most.

Wow! Can you imagine how much hearing that changed my reality? I always thought that I had to get my technique right and that I had to work hard and learn more about the technique and study some more. But no. It is the space that I be that invites others to be and to find what they are looking for.

This awareness matched what I always knew was possible. We can facilitate each other to greater possibilities by simply being present. You know how it is when you talk to someone who has absolutely no judgment of you, who has no point of view that you should change, who is so nurturing and healing. That is the space where you are encouraged to change if and when you choose.

This is how I created Pragmatic Psychology; by asking questions that unlock awareness.

When I meet clients, I ask questions and I embody the questions. I do not buy into the clients' stories, and I look for the things they say that indicate where and how they limit themselves. Limitations are created when people choose unconsciousness and when they choose to be unaware. What truly limits them is often not what they think is limiting them. The change occurs not primarily by talking about the limitation, but by changing the energy. Making the words the source of change is a great limitation. Change is the choice to invite a different possiblity. Shifting the energy and being aware of the choices creates greater ease and expansion; this is what changes people's lives. Letting go of the points of view and judgments people operate from opens up the awareness of what it takes to create what they desire.

You know how you can talk incessantly about a problem and look for the cause and the reasons and all you do is create a story, make the story real, and dig further down into the problem. Your energy is heavy and you usually feel wrong and disenpowered. It is fascinating to me that this is how change is supposed to occur in this reality.

Looking at what expands you and your awareness creates a lightness and an ease in your universe and body, even as you become aware of a negative judgment or a critical attitude that you've been holding.

What if you could be and know and receive the greatness of you. How much of what you call your problems would just disappear and not be relevant anymore? Are you willing to choose to allow your life to be easy and joyful? Where you can receive everything, including you in totality and judge nothing? How much would you like to inspire the world into a different perspective?

By letting go of the wrongness of you, of your pain and suffering, you create a different world. Turning on the lights of awareness and consciousness is where devastation, problems, pain and suffering cannot exist. You cease to be the effect. You are the terminator of pain and suffering; the "pain buster."

Being aware and conscious is where all of life comes to you with ease and joy and glory.

You being and embodying consciousness eliminates the walls of separation between yourself and others; between you and what you truly desire.

Welcome to your world. Welcome to our world. Welcome to a life of ease, joy and glory. Yes, it's a choice you have.

ABOUT THE AUTHOR

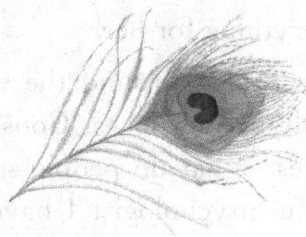

Mag. Susanna Mittermaier, CFMW, licensed clinical psychologist, therapist and Access Consciousness® Facilitator from Vienna, Austria, is creating a new paradigm with psychology and therapy, Pragmatic Psychology, using the revolutionary tools of Access Consciousness®.

Susanna has a different and dynamically transforming perspective on psychological pain and mental illness, going beyond what is currently on the market.

Susanna has been working in psychiatry in Sweden for years and has her own practice treating clients with depression, anxiety, bipolar, ADHD, ADD, autism, Aspergers and other mental diagnoses with remarkable results.

Susanna Mittermaier always desired to empower people to know that they know, to be who they are and to be the choice of a more joyful way of living. In addition to becoming a psychologist, Susanna also studied to become a teacher, philosopher, linguistics and practiced other modalities. Susanna has, since she was a child, looked at the world and wondered why people are so unhappy when living can be so much ease and joy. For a while she forgot her knowing. She knew that had to change! It was time to step up, to be and create what she is truly capable of! At that time, she came in contact with Access Consciousness®, which changed everything for her.

Today, Susanna travels around the world to facilitate sessions and workshops and Access Consciousness® classes in various languages. What do people say... "You are the weirdest, most joyful psychologist I have ever met, I feel insanely sane, my world changed!"

Susanna describes it as psychology helping you to adjust to this reality, and adding consciousness just completely takes you out of the box to access more of you than you could imagine was possible!

PRAGMATIC PSYCHOLOGY CLASSES

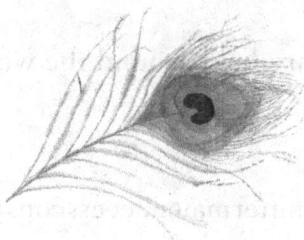

What if there was a different paradigm available for depressions, anxiety, bipolar, eating disorders, schizophrenia and every other clinically diagnosed "disorder"? Susanna Mittermaier, clinical psychologist from Austria knows there is! Susanna has been using the tools of Access Consciousness® in mental health in Sweden and her practice for years and has seen incredible changes. What if you could get over being normal and tap into your true brilliance? What is right about you that you are not getting? And how can you shift what is supposedly only handled over a lifetime and with medication with tools and questions instead?

These classes are for everybody. People who have been diagnosed, their family members, friends, therapists of any kind, parents, teachers, social workers. Everybody who is curious about finding out more about greater possibilities for change and about facilitating change and all of you who are willing to access what You know!

Welcome to going from pain, suffering and gory to ease joy and glory!

Scan for more information

These classes are held around the world and also online.

www.susannamittermaier.accessconsciousness.com

Testimonials:

I'm a psychiatric nurse, and I have been at Susanna's Pragmatic Psychology class. I work with adolescents who have a diagnosed mental illness and support their families to support them. I also have an adult son with schizophrenia. The gift that Susanna brings in her work is an entirely different way to view mental illness; she looks past the stigma that "illness" brings to the gifts and capacities that those children and adults truly possess. She teaches us how to access our own knowing to hold the space for a different possibility for our clients and families and ourselves. And she does it with such lightness and joy! I listen to the audios over and over as I walk to work because it really helps to set such a calm positive tone for the day. Thank-you so much Susanna!

Hello Susanna!

Many thanks for your Pragmatic Psychology class! I am so grateful for you and the class. I listen to it over and over again. I recognize myself in much of what you have done. I work at the school and there are many similarities in the health care system. Your class has begun to open up another possibility in the real world for me to work as a teacher in a different way, a way I know works for me and creates greater possibilities, so THANK YOU from the bottom of my heart

I see a different path now. So what else is possible? You are amazing and, wow, what a contribution to this world and reality!

How it gets even better than this?

Scan for more information

For more information about the author:

www.susannamittermaier.com

ACCESS CONSCIOUSNESS® CORE CLASSES

Access Consciousness® is a set of tools and techniques designed to help you change whatever isn't working in your life, so that you can have a different life and a different reality. Are you ready to explore the infinite possibilities?

The Core Classes listed below can expand your capacity for consciousness so you have greater awareness about you, your life, this reality and beyond! With greater awareness, you can begin generating the life you always knew was possible and haven't yet created. What else is possible? Consciousness includes everything and judges nothing.

~ Gary Douglas, Founder, Access Consciousness®

Access Bars™

The first class in Access Consciousness® is The Bars. Did you know there are 32 points on your head, which when gently touched, effortlessly and easily release the thoughts, ideas, beliefs, emotions and considerations you have stored in any lifetime?

Is your life not yet what you would like it to be? You could have everything you desire (and then some!) if you were willing to receive more and do a little less! Receiving or learning The Bars will allow this—and so much more—to show up for you!

The Bars class is a prerequisite for all Access Consciousness® Core Classes, as it allows your body to process and receive with ease all the changes you are choosing.

Duration: 1 day

Foundation & Level 1

Access Consciousness® is a pragmatic system for functioning beyond the limitations of a world that doesn't work for you. By looking at life's issues from a completely different perspective, it becomes easy to change anything.

Access Foundation is about getting outside the matrix of this reality and uncovering and releasing the points of view that are limiting you.

In Level 1, you will discover how to create your life as you desire it. This class will give you even greater awareness of you as an infinite being and the infinite choices you have available.

Duration: 2 days per class

Prerequisites: Access Bars (and Foundation to do Level 1)

Levels 2 & 3

In these two classes offered by Access Consciousness® founder, Gary Douglas or Dr. Dain Heer, you will gain access to a space where you begin to recognize your capacities as an infinite being. You will become more aware of what you would like to generate as your life: financially, in relationships, in your work and beyond.

Generating your life is a moment-by-moment increase in what is possible in your life. When you stop creating from your past, you can start generating a future that is unlimited. What if sensing the possibilities could replace judgment of everywhere you are right or wrong?

~ Gary Douglas

Duration: 4 days (2 days for Level 2 & 2 days for Level 3)

Prerequisites: Access Bars, Foundation, Level 1

Access Body Class

What if your body was a guide to the secrets, mysteries and magic of life? The Access Body Class was created by Gary Douglas and Dr. Dain Heer and is facilitated by Certified Body Class Facilitators.

The Access Body Class is designed to open up a dialogue and create a communion with your body that allows you to enjoy your body instead of fighting against it. When you change the way you relate to your body, you change the way you relate to everything in your life. People who have attended the Access Body Class have reported dramatic changes in body size and/or shape, relief from chronic and acute pain and greater ease in their relationships and money issues.

Do you have a talent and ability to work with bodies that you haven't yet unlocked? Or are you a body worker, massage therapist, chiropractor, medical doctor or nurse looking for a way to enhance the healing you can do for your clients?

Come play with us and explore how to communicate and relate to bodies, including yours, in many new ways.

Duration: 3 days

Prerequisites: Access Bars, Foundation, Level 1

Advanced Access Body Class with Gary Douglas

This class offers a unique set of new body processes that give your body the possibility of going beyond the limitations of this reality. What if you could undo the limitations locked into your body that create an alteration of the way it functions? What if your body could become far more efficient? What if you and your body didn't have to function the way everyone in this reality believes they have to?

What if food, supplements and exercise have almost nothing to do with how your body truly functions? What if you could have ease, joy and communion with your body far beyond what is considered possible right now? Would you be willing to explore the possibilities?

Duration: 3 days

Prerequisites: Access Bars, Foundation, Levels 1, 2 & 3 & the 3-day Access Body Class two times

The Symphony of Possibilities with Dr. Dain Heer

What if you are the composer of your reality? What if you have the capacity to be the maestro of the Universe? Is it time to become what you were *always* meant to be?

This evening class is the very beginning of the *The Symphony of Possibilities,* an advanced training where you become intimately aware of energies and learn how to truly utilize them to create your life, living and a totally different reality.

What if WE, acoustically vibrating as us, create an energetic *symphony of possibilities* that changes the world and the planet?

The Symphony of Possibilities—Advanced Training with Dr. Dain Heer

Introducing *The Symphony of Possibilities*, a 3.5 day advanced training where you become intimately aware of energies and learn how to truly utilize them to create your life, living and a totally different reality.

Are you aware that your capacities with energies are *unique*? Do you know that the way you resonate with the world is a fantastic, phenomenal and an absolute *gift*? Are you ready to step into and BE all of that now?

This is a training like no other! Dain uses his energetic transformation process, the Energetic Synthesis of Being, to open up the space of infinite possibilities and invites you to discover your capacities by working energetically on other people in the class.

With the facilitation of Dain, and together with the group, you begin to access all that is truly available to you. What if WE, acoustically vibrating as us, create an energetic *symphony of possibilities* that changes the world and the planet?

Duration: 3 1/2 days

Prerequisites: Bars, Foundation, Level 1, 2 & 3

Being You, Changing the World—The Beginning with Dr. Dain Heer

This one-evening class, which is open to everyone, will give you a taste of what else is possible in your life. It is also the beginning of the 2½ Day Being You, Changing the World Class.

Access Consciousness® 7-Day Events

Are you an adventurer and a seeker of ever-greater possibilities? Are you willing to consider questions you've never asked before? And are you ready to receive more change than you can imagine? If so, the 7-day event just might be for you!

These invitation-only, freeform classes are held twice a year in beautiful locations around the world by Access Consciousness® founder, Gary Douglas. To be invited, you must have attended at least one Level 2 & 3 class in person.

There is no other class or event like this offered anywhere in the world. It is a unique and life-changing experience.

Prequisites: Level 2 and 3

Duration: 7 days

To find out more about Access Consciousness® classes see: www.accessconsciousness.com

OTHER ACCESS CONSCIOUSNESS®
PUBLISHING BOOKS

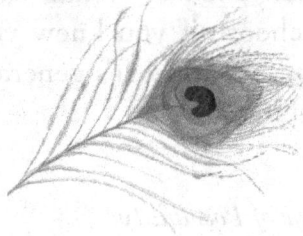

Divorceless Relationships
By Gary M. Douglas

Most of us spend a lot of time divorcing parts and pieces of ourselves in order to care for someone else. For example, you like to go jogging but instead of jogging, you spend that time with your partner to show him or her that you really care. "I love you so much that I would give up this thing that is valuable to me so I can be with you." This is one of the ways you divorce you to create an intimate relationship. How often does divorcing you really work in the long run?

Being You, Changing the World
By Dr. Dain Heer

Have you always known that something COMPLETE-LY DIFFERENT is possible? What if you had a handbook for infinite possibilities and dynamic change to guide you? With tools and processes that actually worked and invited you to a completely different way of being? For you? And the world?

Joy of Business
By Simone Milasas

If you were creating your business from the JOY of it—what would you choose? What would you change? What would you choose if you knew you could not fail? Business is JOY, it's creation, it's generative. It can be the adventure of LIVING.

Leading from the Edge of Possibility:
No More Business as Usual
By Chutisa and Steven Bowman

This book is for people who are dedicated to creating a life greater than what they now have and to making a difference in the world. In this book, *Leading from the Edge of Possibility,* authors Chutisa and Steven Bowman provide insights into business and life that have arisen out of their work with thousands of executive boards and teams over several decades.

The subject of this book is no more business as usual. But perhaps more precisely it is a book about possibility, choice, question, contribution and what it would take to lead your business and your life from the edge of infinite possibility.

For more Access Consciousness® Books go to
www.accessconsciousnesspublishing.com

Scan for more information

www.ingramcontent.com/pod-product-compliance
Lightning Source LLC
Chambersburg PA
CBHW010144270326
41928CB00018B/3244